CW01663446

We would like to thank everyone in the production team for their contributions. Camilla for the photographs, Zoe for the design, Thérèse for the editing and Toni for the cartoons - we couldn't have done it without you!
Thanks
Helen and Linda

dye one **knit** one

ISBN 978-0-9540333-7-8 spiral bound
ISBN 978-0-9540333-8-5 thread sewn
© Helen Deighan / Linda de Ruiter 2009

Illustrations by © Toni Goffe 2009

Photography by Camilla Blackie
www.camillabackie.com

Designed by A couple of jugs creative agency
www.acoupleofjugs.com

Edited by Thérèse Tobin

The rights of Helen Deighan, Linda de Ruiter and Toni Goffe to be identified as the authors and illustrator of this work have been asserted by them in accordance with the Copyright, Design and Patents Act 1988.

First published in Great Britain 2009

10 9 8 7 6 5 4 3 2 1

All rights reserved. No part of this publication may be reproduced, stored in a retrieval system, or transmitted, in any form or by any means, without the prior written permission of the publisher, nor be otherwise circulated in any form of binding or cover than that in which it is published and without a similar condition being imposed on the subsequent purchaser.

Published by Crossways Patch
Rose Glen, Crossways Road, Grayshott,
Hindhead, Surrey GU26 6HG
www.crosswayspatch.co.uk

Printed and bound by Midas Press, Columbus Drive, Southwood, Farnborough, Hampshire GU14 0NZ

A CIP record is registered by and held at the British Library

Toni Goffe illustrator extraordinaire.
Toni has delighted many readers of my books over the years with his delightful cat cartoons. Go to www.tonigoffe.com to see more of his work.

acknowledgements

dye one knit one

Helen Deighan and Linda De Ruiter

contents

"The purest and most thoughtful minds are those which love colour the most"
– John Ruskin

Knitting was my first creative pursuit. I learned by sitting on my grandmother's knee at the age of four - first just putting the yarn round the needle, then putting the needle through the loop, and so on until I had mastered all the moves. I won my first competition at the age of seven with a knitted hot-water-bottle cover. I knitted like crazy all through my teenage years. Then when I went away to college and discovered all the other 'textiley' things that were on offer, my knitting needles were put on the back boiler - until NOW!

I am completely hooked again thanks to my friend and colleague Linda de Ruiter, who has shown me just how exciting knitting can be. When I was doing patchwork in the 80s, I soon decided I wanted to dye my own fabrics and the same thing has happened with knitting. I want to dye my own yarn - and of course not with just one colour.

Dyeing in Plastic Bags, my first book written in 2001, gave instructions for dyeing cotton fabric. This book has been, and continues to be, very popular because I made dyeing easy, clean and accessible, particularly to those people who were a little nervous and had not done it before. I wanted, therefore, to do the same for knitters. It really is true that dyeing can be very simple - in fact if you can cook a meal, you can dye some yarn.

When I was writing the dyeing part of this book, I soon realised that a lot of the text was repeated. I know people don't like seeing "look on page 96" etc., particularly when the have their hands in dye! Zoe, our wonderful designer, came up with the brilliant idea of having flaps, one at the front for dyeing information and one at the back for knitting info. So when you are following the dyeing instructions for example, open the front flap before you start then you can easily look at it every time you see this sign.

The same applies if you are following one of the knitting patterns but this time open the back flap.

In this book I have written the section on dyeing and Linda has created some wonderful patterns in the knitting section. You can of course buy yarn and just use the patterns but I hope you will also have a go at the dyeing - it really is easier than you think.

Good luck, have fun - and remember, disasters can always be dyed again.

Helen

If I could write this intro with a pair of knitting needles in my hands, I probably would. Not because I don't want to write, but because I don't associate knitting with writing. I will explain.

I have knitted as long as I can remember. My mum used to sew a lot of our clothes (as well as her own). As soon as I was old enough (about 7 or 8), I was given my own little sewing machine and I started making clothes for my dolls. I started knitting in that same period. Since I am left-handed, my mum taught me by sitting opposite me, so I could mirror her moves. The oldest piece of knitting I can remember was a red skirt for one of my Barbies.

By the time I started secondary school, I had moved on from making dolls' clothes to making my own. And my knitting moved up a gear as well. I soon found out that knitting in the opposite direction brought its own set of challenges when knitting more complicated patterns. So I taught myself to knit in the other direction, which works a treat as long as I hold my needles in a different position - a very awkward position, from a right-handed knitter's perspective! It opened up a whole new world for me, though, and I knitted throughout my teenage years as well as at college. My dad recalls that my parents often thought I was studying in my bedroom, only to find out I was knitting (again!). He managed to keep his ongoing worries about this hidden though, so my obsession gradually blossomed to the point of knitting an average of one jumper a week.

Back to the writing though: I always tended to use a knitting pattern for inspiration and as a motivator to buy yarn, but once I started knitting, I'd never follow the pattern and I'd make my own modifications. All my designs were one-offs, because I NEVER wrote anything down.

And there's the crunch: my biggest challenge for this book was to move away from quirky one-offs to creating patterns that not only showcase Helen's nifty dyeing techniques, but that are easy to understand and knit.

Well, the first batch of patterns I've written as a result of our collaboration is here. I hope you'll enjoy them as much as I have enjoyed creating them, because if it's up to us, there'll be plenty more to come!

Linda

chapter one

basic requirements

Along with the dishes, jars and cling film (listed at the beginning of each chapter), you will also need dye, a heat source and, of course, yarn, which are all quite specific to this type of dyeing.

acid dye

Don't be alarmed by the name - you will not be mixing up vast vats of fuming acid baths, like a scene from a Hammer Horror movie.

The 'acid' in acid dye refers to a bit of white vinegar (the colourless version of malt vinegar) or citric acid which is used in the dyeing process – both quite harmless. The dyes themselves are non-caustic and even non-toxic in some cases, as these are actually used in food colouring. I would not, however, suggest you try drinking the stuff! There are different types of acid dye – levelling, milling and super milling – but all you really need to remember is the acid bit.

Acid dyes are used to dye protein fibres – that is anything that has been grown by an animal, such as wool, angora, cashmere, possum, alpaca, silk. They will also, surprisingly enough, dye nylon, but not acrylic. They come in powder form and, as with any dye, must be treated with some respect when in this form: when mixed with water, however, they are perfectly safe. Disposal is also easy as the yarn will absorb all the dye, leaving a clear liquid which does no harm to anything.

For the purposes of this book, I would suggest using either an acid dye which is sold as such and requires vinegar, or an All-in-one acid dye which has everything you need in the pot so you only need to add water. This is a very convenient way of buying dye, although a little more expensive. (See page 96 for a list of suppliers.)

Don't expect all dyes to behave in exactly the same ways. Different colours have different characteristics and it is good to be aware of this. Not wishing to become too technical, I have listed a few of the characteristics of the dyes that have been used in this book.

Autumn Sky – this mixes into quite a 'thick' liquid and when left to go cold, goes quite gloopy – a bit like un-set jelly. This disappears when it is heated again.

Turmeric, Paprika, Charcoal and Winter Red are all very strong dyes. In fact you can halve the quantities and still get a good dye. Just be aware of this strength when mixing these with other colours.

Pale Pumpkin and Sage both mix to a very thin solution. They are, however, very quick to react. This means it is quite difficult to get an even coverage, particularly when using the microwave or steam.

Plum mixes to a thin solution but don't be fooled, this is a strong dye and will take over whenever it can.

Stone, Lemon Yellow,* Slate and Spring Yellow mix to thin solutions and are quite quick to react, although an even coverage can be acquired with lots of squidging and squeezing with a gloved hand.

Turquoise* is quite slow to react – you may need to add vinegar or citric acid solution to the rinsing water to get rid of the colour completely.

Cerise* is quite hard to mix into a good solution. There always seems to be a sediment. This means you must give it a good stir before using it.

Summer Green mixes well but needs to be squidged quite quickly to get an even coverage.

In this book we have been using, for the most part, 'All-in-one' dyes (see suppliers list on page 96).

Acid milling dyes (marked with a *) were used for mixing colours in chapter 04 as they are a bit stronger and behave well when mixed together.

Procion MX dyes can be used in any of the techniques explained in the book, but the colours might not be as strong.

the funny things that some dyes do

heat source

Heat is required to make acid dyes work. You can use various methods:

Some dyeing techniques require different methods of applying heat which you will discover as you go through the book.

01 microwave oven

I find that the quickest and easiest method is to use a microwave oven.

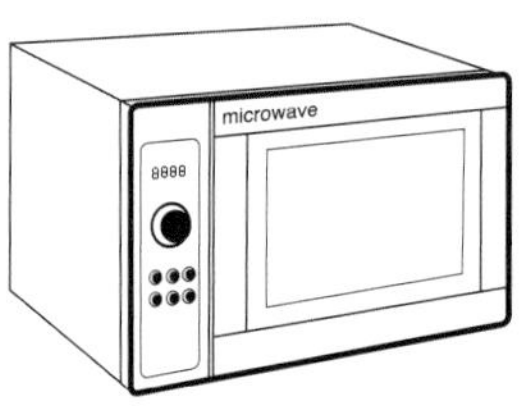

Domestic microwaves are normally about 600 – 750 watts. The highest setting is too hot, and I find the 'medium' to 'medium/low' setting the best to use.

I keep an old microwave just for dyeing. Although this is not essential, I would recommend you try and pick up a cheap model if you intend doing a lot of dyeing using this method. The most basic of ovens will suffice.

02 steam

If you do not own or would prefer not to use a microwave oven, there is an alternative. Fibre can be steamed either in a steamer or in a colander over a pan of boiling water.

03 immersion

Fibre can also be dyed in a pan on the stove. You have to be careful not to let it boil. Bring the liquid up to near boiling point – that is, steam rising and the pan is singing, but no bubbles! If you have a thermometer, the correct temperature is about 80° centigrade.

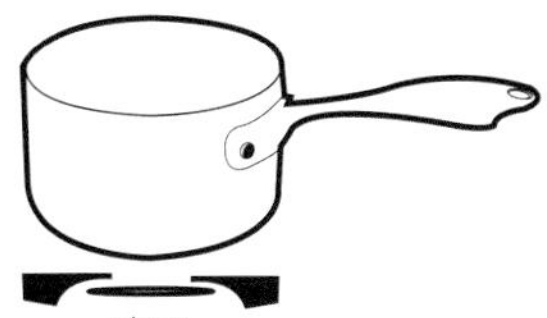

vinegar or citric acid

The easiest type of acid to get hold of is white vinegar but if you can't stand the smell (I can't), then use citric acid crystals dissolved in water. These are used in making wine and beer and I find home brewing specialists good places to buy quantities very cheaply. (See page 96 for a list of suppliers.)

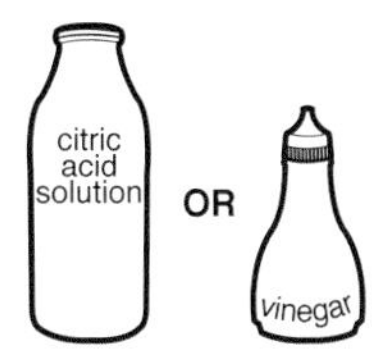

to make a citric acid solution

Dissolve 100 grams of citric acid crystals in 1 litre of very hot water.
Store in a suitable container – an old plastic drinks bottle is ideal.
Because citric acid is a natural substance, it can go off. To avoid this, label the bottle and store it in the refrigerator and it will last for a couple of weeks.

fibre facts

Fibre content is one of the most important considerations when choosing the best yarn for your project. It determines how to care for it but also how it drapes once knitted, the way it looks and feels and most importantly: if and how you can dye it!

This book focuses on the use of acid dyes to colour knitting yarns. Acid dyes are suitable for dyeing protein fibres. All animal fibres are protein fibres. Protein has a specific cell structure that is different from the cell structure of most plant fibres. However, there now are some plant-derived fibres that behave as protein fibres. And nylon (a synthetic) does as well.

So how do you know which fibres you can dye with acid dyes?
To avoid (or alleviate!) confusion, below is a grid that shows you which fibre belongs where. If you come across a fibre that is not covered by the list, do let us know!

Of course there are many blended fibres around as well. If you've never dyed yarn before, then (if possible) keep it simple by choosing a yarn that is either 100% one fibre, or a blend that primarily consists of one fibre. If you do use a blend, then the result of your dyeing efforts may differ, depending on the type of blend.

Examples: a wool/nylon blend will dye very well, as both fibres in the blend like acid dyes. A wool/cotton blend is likely to come out lighter than an all-wool yarn, as the acid dye will take well on the wool but not on the cotton. Then there may be pleasant surprises too, e.g. when dyeing a wool/tencel blend with acid dye. The tencel takes the acid dye better than you would expect but you will achieve a more muted result than when you use the same dye on a pure wool.

The golden rule here is: when in doubt, do a dye test by dyeing a small amount of yarn (as little as a yard) in the microwave, using only a spoonful of dye solution. It won't take long and it rules out any unpleasant surprises!

* Some synthetic fibres can only be dyed using disperse dyes. Since this can only be done at very high temperatures, this process is not feasible at home.
** Spandex/Lycra/Elastane do not withstand high temperatures, as these may affect their elasticity. They'll be happy in a plant-fibre blend, as Procion dyeing is a cold dyeing process. But beware of these fibres in any acid dye baths, as they may lose their elasticity completely!
A bit more about the fibres in the grid...

fibre	acid dye	procion mix	dye? don't try!
animal fibres			
wool	●		
silk	●		
angora	●		
mohair	●		
cashmere	●		
alpaca / llama / camel	●		
azlon fibres [regenerated protein]			
corn [ingeo]	●		
soy silk [tofu]	●		
milk protein [silk latte]	●		
plant fibres			
cotton		●	
linen / flax		●	
hemp / sisal / jute / raffia		●	
bamboo		●	
cellulose fibres			
modal		●	
rayon / viscos		●	
ramie		●	
tencel / lyocell		●	
synthetic fibres			
nylon / polyamide	●		
polyester			●
spandex / lycra / elastane			●
acrylic			●

animal fibres

WOOL
Spun from the fleece of sheep, wool is versatile, durable and elastic. Its unique properties allow a garment made of wool to retain its shape and it won't wrinkle easily. It makes for a good insulating layer, which helps the body to regulate its temperature. Wool can absorb up to one-third of its weight before it feels wet to the touch. That works both in hot and cold conditions, turning it into a multi-climate fibre of choice. Wool can be felted by applying friction, moisture and heat, which is how it has gained a reputation for being difficult to wash. The trick is to avoid friction, so for most wool, a standard cycle in a washing machine is not good (lots of friction!). But soaking it in warm water with a wool-wash detergent and putting it in the washing machine for a spin cycle only is fine. Lay it flat to dry rather than chucking it in the dryer, as the dryer is another combination of friction and heat. If a wool yarn is called "superwash", it has been treated to lose its felting properties. This is great when home-dyeing, but make sure not to use a superwash yarn when you want to felt. Superwash yarns are especially popular amongst sock knitters as they eliminate the chance of your precious hard work going to waste in the washing machine.

ANGORA
Angora fibres are harvested from angora rabbits. It is extremely soft, fluffy and warm. One angora rabbit can yield about 300 grams of fibre once every 3 months, depending on the quality of the angora. French angora rabbits are known to produce the highest yields. Because angora is so expensive, it is often blended with other fibres, which also makes it easier to spin and limits the fibres to shed (as they are not that long).

MOHAIR
Mohair is the fleece from the angora goat. The finest mohair comes from the kids ("kid mohair"). It is extremely soft and unique in its feel.

CASHMERE
Cashmere is also harvested from goats - the Chinese and Tibetan cashmere goats. They live in hard-to-reach, mountainous areas and the cashmere can only be harvested once a year by combing it from the goats' bellies.

ALPACA / LLAMA / CAMEL
Grouped together because these are all animals from the camel family, these fibres are steadily growing in popularity, and with good reason. They are luxurious, soft and warm as well as lightweight. And because they are hollow fibres, they insulate really well.

azlon fibres

These are all manufactured fibres. They are made by converting the protein generated from the various sources into a solution that is extruded through the holes of a "spinneret". They are then stretched to improve the alignment of the chains of molecules that make up the fibres. Protein from both animal and vegetable sources can be used. Azlon fibres are soft and warm, absorb moisture, do not accumulate static electricity and do not felt. They are often used in blends and are gaining popularity as hand-knitting yarns.

plant fibres

COTTON
Cotton is grown all over the world. It absorbs moisture, dries easily and is non-allergenic. It is easy to wash and it can be treated with different finishes to change its appearance. The most widely used treatment is called "mercerising", after its inventor, a Scot called John Mercer. The process involves treating the cotton with caustic soda and stretching it to make it smoother, stronger and less prone to shrinking. This gives the cotton sheen. Don't let the mention of caustic soda fool you: it is considered environmentally friendly and low impact compared with the processes involved in making some of the fibres produced by chemical processing. There are different grades of cotton. The finest grade is commonly known as "Egyptian Cotton".

LINEN / FLAX
Linen is made by spinning fibres from the stems of flax into a strong yarn. Like cotton, it is easy to wash and comfortable to wear in warm weather, as it absorbs moisture quickly. Knitted linen is popular for its lovely elasticity and drape. In knitting yarn, linen is often blended with cotton, to make the resulting yarn softer.

HEMP / SISAL / JUTE / RAFFIA

These are all plant fibres that are heavier than linen and coarser in their feel. They have been widely used for centuries to make twine, rope and sackcloth, as they are very hard-wearing and strong. Hemp is steadily gaining in popularity as a knitting yarn, both in its pure form and in blends.

BAMBOO

Bamboo is in essence a grass. Although the outer wall of the stems is very hard, the leaves and the inner pith of the stems are easy to pulp and process into a fibre by crushing and mixing with caustic soda. It is not difficult to understand why bamboo has gained popularity so fast, as it is durable, absorbent, keeps you warm, is anti-bacterial, has superb drapery and dyes well. Bamboo yarns are here to stay!

cellulose fibres

MODAL

Modal is the generic name for all man-made cellulose fibres. It is made from high quality wooden pulps. It is strong yet soft and shiny and remains so when washed frequently. It is ideal for clothes because it breathes so well. Because it absorbs up to 50% more moisture than cotton, it is very popular for use in fitness outfits.

RAYON / VISCOSE

This fibre may be man-made, but it is not considered synthetic as it is spun, either as a filament or staple, from cellulose obtained from cotton lint and wood chips. Rayon tends to be shinier and softer than cotton and dyes extremely well, achieving a vibrancy of colour that is hard to surpass.

RAMIE

Ramie is a bit like linen and most widely used in the Orient. It is strong, lustrous and washes well. It is a little stiff and is often blended with other fibres.

TENCEL / LYOCELL

Tencel is the brand name for lyocell, made from wood pulp. It is owned by Courtaulds, the original producer of rayon, who modified its manufacturing process to produce Tencel. The production process is very environmentally friendly, contributing to its astronomical rise in popularity. That is not its only claim to fame though: it breathes and absorbs like a natural fibre, is durable and easy to care for like a man-made fibre, and achieves a smoothness and drape that surpasses all others. It can be washed and dried, retains shape and colour, and dyes very readily, achieving the vibrancy of rayon.

synthetic fibres

NYLON / POLYAMIDE

Nylon was the brand name for polyamide produced by Du Pont but has become the generic name for polyamide. Nylon is very strong and durable and the only synthetic fibre that takes acid dyes (the dyes used to dye animal fibre). In knitting yarn, nylon is used a lot to strengthen wool yarn, e.g. to produce hard-wearing sock yarns.

POLYESTER

Very easy to care for and very wrinkle resistant, polyester holds its shape well, even when wet (most non-iron garments contain a percentage of polyester). As with nylon, it is often added to other fibres to give extra strength and durability.

SPANDEX / LYCRA/ELASTANE

Lycra is a brand name for spandex or elastane, a synthetic fibre known for its exceptional elasticity. It is stronger and more durable than rubber, a non-synthetic alternative. It was invented in 1959 by Du Pont. When used in knitting yarns, it's present in a small percentage to give the yarns more elasticity and help them hold their shape. It cannot withstand high temperatures and does not take dyes unless a specialised industrial dyeing process is used.

ACRYLIC

Acrylics look like wool but are synthetic. They can have great bounce and be very soft to the touch, but they don't have the insulating properties of wool. They are often present in wool blends. Acrylics can only be dyed using very high temperature and disperse dyes. These conditions cannot be achieved when dyeing at home, so when dyeing a wool/acrylic blend, do expect a paler end result and don't try to dye 100% acrylic yarn.

chapter two

01. 

02. 

03. 

04. 

05. 

06. 

07. 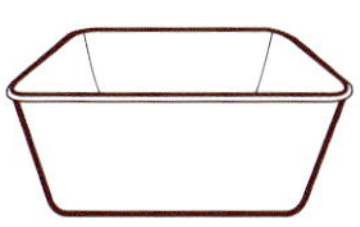

08. 

OR

09. 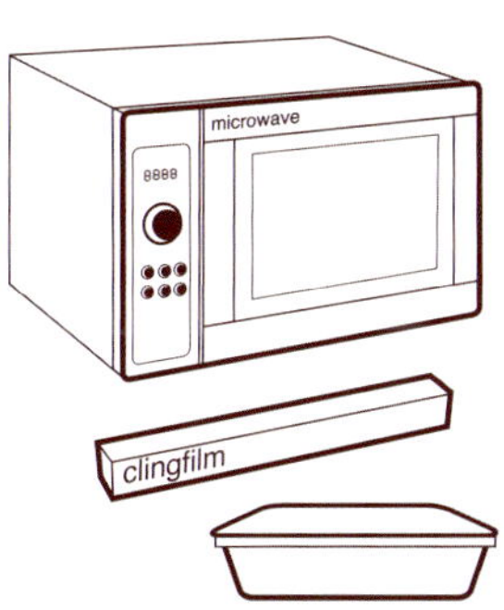

the quick and easy way!

I think this method of dyeing is one of the easiest. It is also very quick for those of you (like me) who are impatient to see your results. As it is all done in the microwave, you are limited to about 100 grams of dry weight yarn in each dye bath.

you will need

01. Dye powder
02. Measuring spoons
03. A glass jar and a spoon for mixing
04. Boiling water
05. 100 grams of yarn (protein fibres or nylon)
06. White vinegar or citric acid solution if not using 'All-in-one' acid dyes
07. A bowl for soaking
08. A steamer and 'boil-in-a-bag' plastic bags
OR
09. A microwave oven and a dish with a lid (cling film can be used in place of a lid)

preparing the dye solution

For 100 grams of yarn dry weight you will need 100ml of dye solution.

TIP

Always take care when handling dye powder.

preparing the yarn

Wind the yarn into a hank, if it has come as a ball. Secure the hank in 4-5 places with a figure-of-eight-knot (see below). I try and use acrylic yarn for this as it is then easy to spot after the hank is dyed (acrylic yarn will not take the dye). The yarn must then be soaked.

the dyeing process

using a microwave oven

01. Remove the yarn from the soaking bowl and place (still dripping) in a suitable dish.

02. Add 100ml of dye solution. Gently move and squeeze the yarn to help the dye get to all parts - try not to leave any white bits, unless, of course, that is the effect you are after.

03. Cover the dish with a lid. making sure no yarn is exposed. Either leave one corner of the lid slightly open or pierce the lid with a few holes to allow steam to escape while cooking.

04. Place in the microwave for 10 minutes on medium heat. Check after 5 minutes to make sure no yarn is drying out. If it is, turn the hank until it is all wet again. Be careful as the fibres and liquid will be very hot. Return to the microwave for the final 5 minutes.

Take the dish out of the oven and carefully remove the lid. Check the residue liquid. This should be clear or pale by now. If it is still quite dark, replace the lid as before and 'cook' for another 5 minutes on medium heat.

05. Leave to cool completely. Any dye that is left in the residue liquid will be absorbed during this time.

TIP To get a really even coverage, try putting the dye with a litre of warm water in a large bowl (a washing up bowl will do) Then add the hank of yarn and swish it around before transferring the whole lot, liquid and hank, to a smaller bowl or jug that will go in the microwave. Cover with cling film and microwave as before.

01.

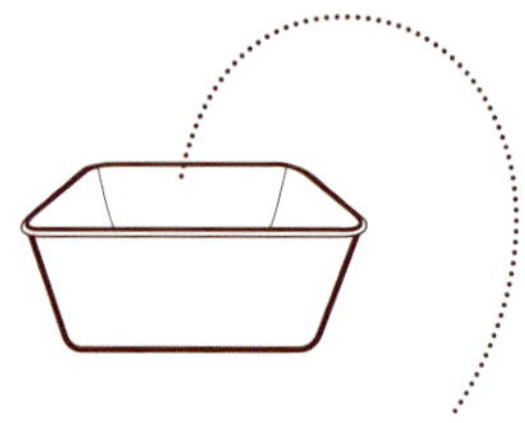

02.

03.

04.

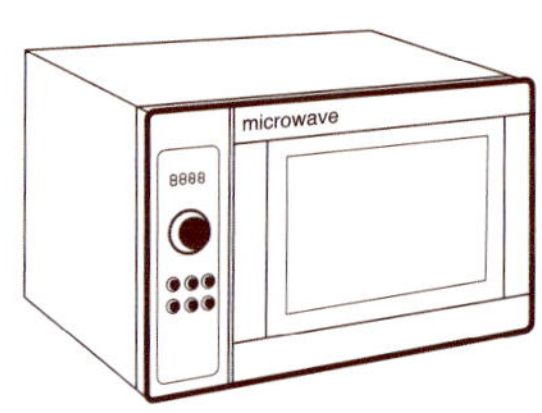

05.

using a steamer

01. Remove the hank from the soaking bowl and place in a good quality plastic bag (boil-in-a-bag bags are excellent).

02. Add 100ml of dye solution. Gently move and squeeze the yarn to help the dye get to all parts - try not to leave any white bits, unless, of course, that is the effect you are after.

03. Place the bag in a steamer or in a colander over a pan of boiling water.

04. Cover with a lid and steam for 30 - 40 minutes.

05. Leave to cool.

01.
02.
03.
04.
05.

rinsing and drying

Once dyed, all yarn must be given a quick rinse before drying.

Then you can start knitting!

chapter three

01.

02.

03.

04.
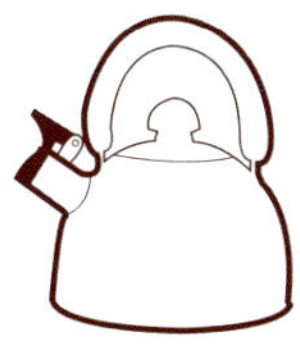

05.
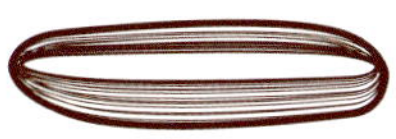

06.

07.
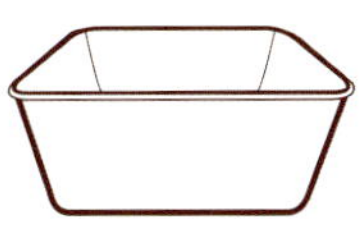

08.
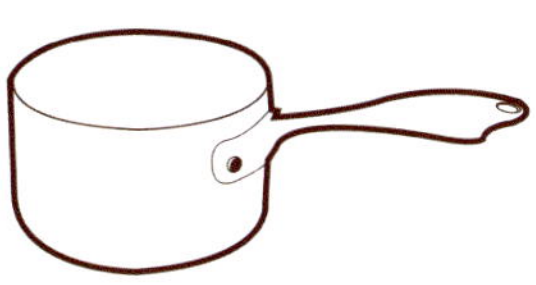

immersion dyeing

This is a different type of dyeing from the techniques covered so far in this book. In this method the yarn is completely immersed in the dye and heated on the stove top.
One great advantage of this type of dyeing is that you can get a very even coverage of colour.

you will need

01. Dye powder
02. Measuring spoons
03. A glass jar and spoon for mixing
04. Boiling water
05. Yarn
06. White vinegar or citric acid solution if not using the 'All-in-one' acid dye
07. A bowl for soaking
08. A large pan - (not aluminium as this affects the dye - stainless steel is best)

The size of the pan depends, of course on the amount of yarn you are dyeing.
As a gauge for 100 grams of yarn you would need at least a 10 litre pan if you want the yarn to be evenly dyed.
Smaller pans can be used, but the yarn will not be dyed quite so evenly.

preparing the dye solution

I find it easier to first make the dye powder into a solution with just 100 ml of water, no matter the amount of dye powder. You can then make sure the powder is thoroughly dissolved before it goes into the pan.

preparing the yarn

Wind the yarn into a hank, if it has come as a ball. Secure the hank in 4-5 places with a figure-of-eight knot. I try and use acrylic yarn for this as it is then easy to spot after the hank is dyed (acrylic yarn will not take the dye). The yarn must then be soaked.

the dyeing process

01. For 100 grams of yarn (dry weight) put about 8 litres of warm water into a pan.

02. Add the dye solution and stir.

03. Remove the yarn from the soaking bowl and gently put it in the pan of warm dye water. Stir (very gently, as too much agitation can cause felting) and just make sure all parts of the hank have absorbed the dye equally. Bring the pan slowly up to temperature.

The exact temperature required is 80° centigrade. But if you don't have a thermometer, don't worry, this is just below boiling point. Steam will be rising, the pan will be singing but no big bubbles have appeared.

Keep at this temperature for 30 - 40 minutes. When the 30 - 40 minutes is up, take the pot off the heat.

The water should now be clear or very pale. If it isn't, all is not lost! Put the pan back on the heat and add a couple of tablespoons of either white vinegar or citric acid solution to the pot. Heat up to dyeing point again and leave for 10 minutes. This should help with the total exhaustion of the dye.

Allow the pot and contents to cool.

TIP

Don't worry if the temperature goes up and down a little - just DON'T let it boil. If it looks as though it is nearing boiling point - that is the bubbles rising are getting bigger and the singing is getting louder - remove the pot from the heat source and allow to cool down a bit. Turn the heat source down a little and after about 5 minutes, return the pot to the heat.

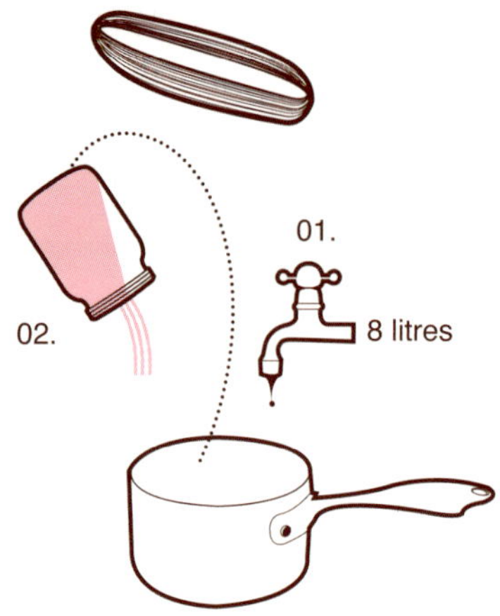

03.

RINSING AND DRYING
Once dyed, all yarn must be given a quick rinse before drying.

Then you can start knitting!

variations

MAKING STRIPES

Make a long hank by winding the yarn around two chairs up-ended on a table.

Secure the hank in 5 or 6 places with a figure-of-eight knot.

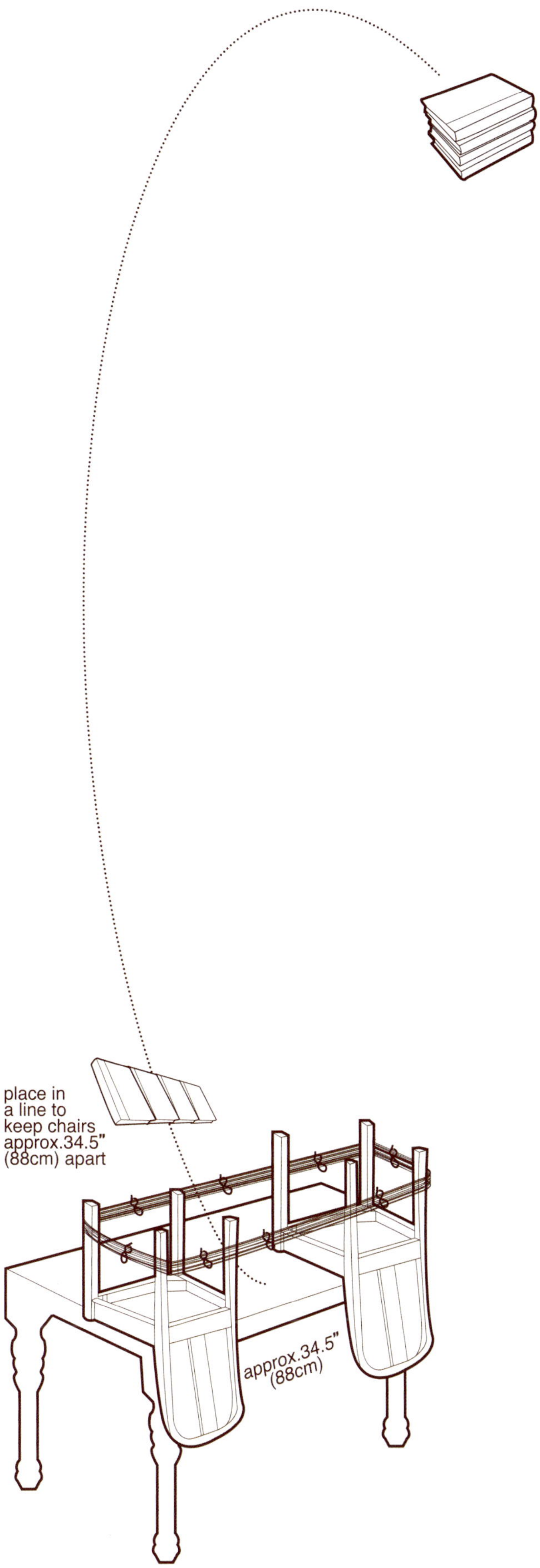

After soaking, gently squeeze the hank to remove excess liquid. Then, gently, either suspend the hank over the pan of dye liquid so that half the hank is submerged, or, if it is easier, put half the hank in the pan and the other half in another empty pan alongside.

When the dyeing process is complete, remove, rinse and dry the yarn and then do the same with the other half using a different colour.

TIP

As you wind the yarn, the chairs are inclined to move towards each other so I put 4 hardback books between them on the table, and this keeps them in place.

MIXING COLOURS

Version one
After soaking, put the hank into a pan containing just water.

THEN add the dye solution.
Use two different colours - allow the dyes to mix a little but not too much. Bring up to temperature and continue as before.

Version two
Add one dye solution to the pan with warm water.

Add yarn and bring it up to temperature. After 10 minutes, add the second colour. This should be a much weaker solution. Do not stir, just allow the second colour to sink down through the yarn.

pink in first followed by yellow

yellow in first followed by pink and stirred

yellow in first followed by pink not stirred

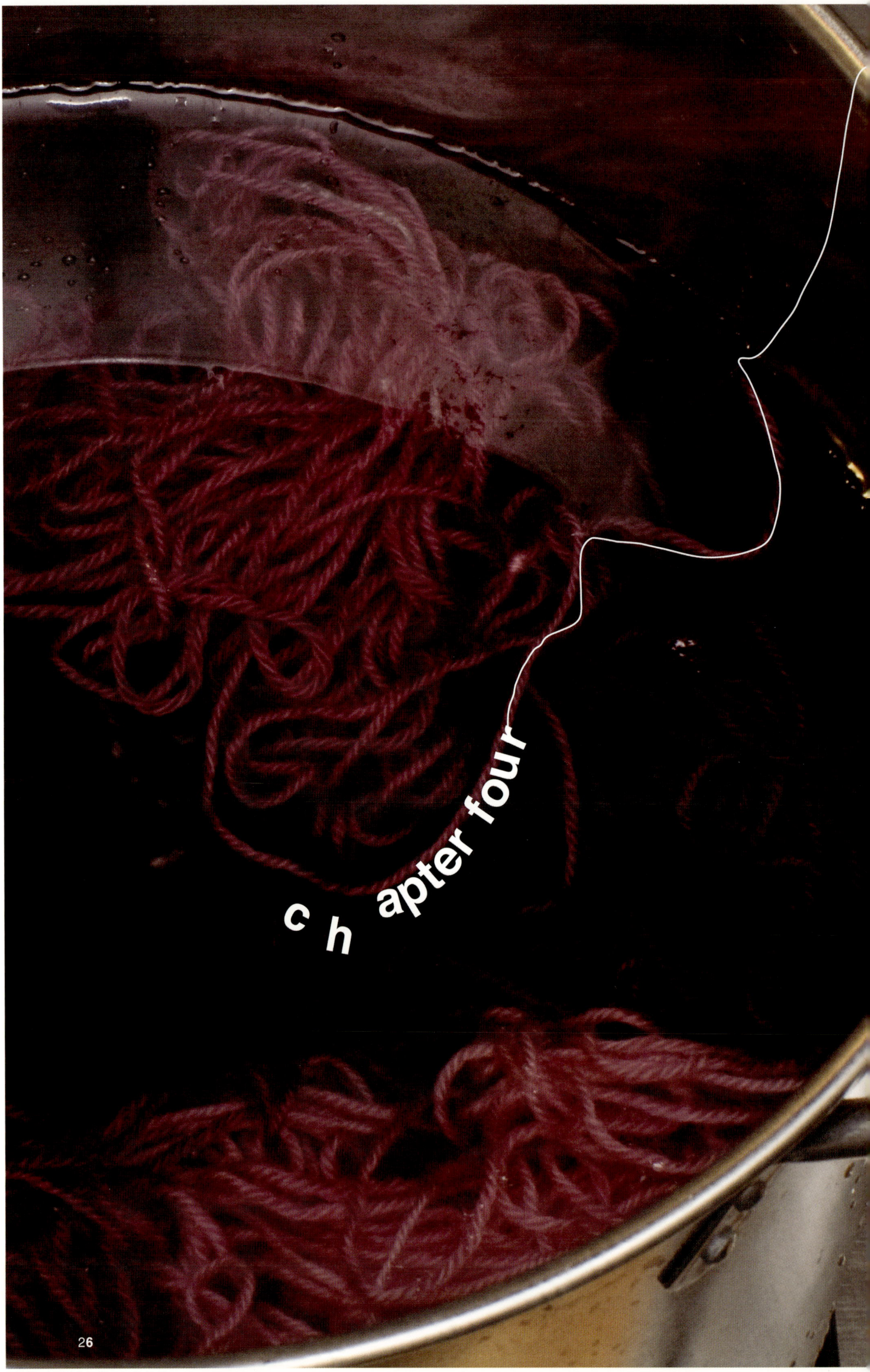
chapter four

01.

02.

03.

04.

05.
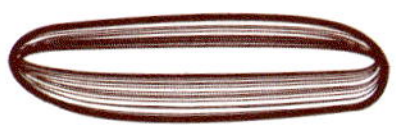

06.

07.
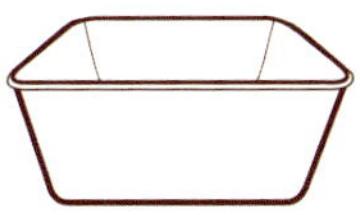

08.
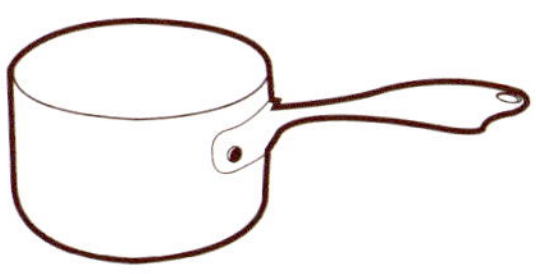

graduated dyeing

This is a method of dyeing yarn using just one colour but varying the shades. Yarn is dyed using the immersion technique.

you will need

01. Dye powder
02. Measuring spoons
03. A glass jar and spoon for mixing
04. Boiling water
05. Yarn
06. White vinegar or citric acid solution if not using the All-in-one acid dye
07. A bowl for soaking
08. A large pan (not aluminium, as this affects the dye - stainless steel is best)
The size of the pan depends, of course, on the amount of yarn you are dyeing.
As a gauge, for 100 grams of yarn, you would need at least a 10-litre pan if you want the yarn to be evenly dyed.
Smaller pans can be used, but the yarn will not be dyed quite so evenly.

preparing the dye solution

Make sure the dye powder is thoroughly dissolved before it goes into the pan.

preparing the yarn

The yarn must be divided into equal hanks.
The example here is to dye 100 grams of yarn (dry weight) in 5 shades.

Divide the yarn into 20-gram hanks. Secure each hank with a couple of figure-of-eight knots. I try and use acrylic yarn for this as it is then easy to spot after the hank is dyed. (acrylic yarn will not take the dye)

The yarn must then be soaked.

the dyeing process

01. For 100 grams of yarn (dry weight) put about 8 litres of warm water into a pan.
02. Add the 100ml of dye solution and stir.
03. Remove one hank of yarn from the soaking bowl and gently put it in the pan of warm dye water.

Stir (very gently, as too much agitation can cause felting) and just make sure all parts of the hank have absorbed the dye equally.
Bring the pan slowly up to temperature.
The exact temperature required is 80° centigrade. But if you don't have a thermometer, don't worry, this is just below boiling point. Steam will be rising, the pan will be singing but no big bubbles have appeared.
When the pan has reached the right temperature, set a kitchen timer for 5 minutes. Or just look at the clock!

04. When 5 minutes is up, add the second hank of yarn to the pan.

Repeat this, adding one hank every five minutes until all the hanks are in the pan.

Leave for another 5 minutes before taking the pan off the heat.

The water should now be clear or very pale.
Allow the pan and contents to cool.

TIP

Don't worry if the temperature goes up and down a little - just DON'T let it boil. If it looks as though it is nearing boiling point - that is the bubbles rising are getting bigger and the singing is getting louder - remove the pot from the heat source and allow to cool down a bit. Turn the heat source down a little and after about 5 minutes, return the pot to the heat.

01.

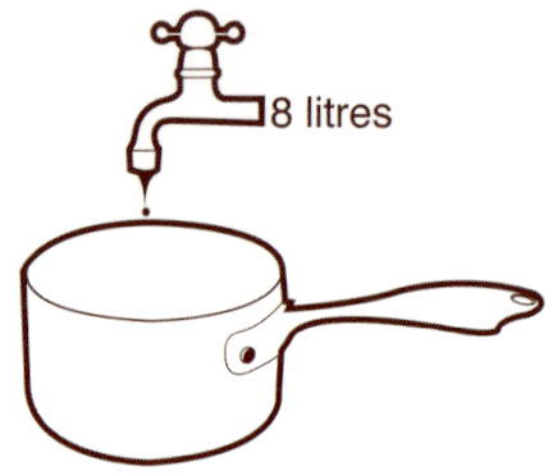

02.

03.

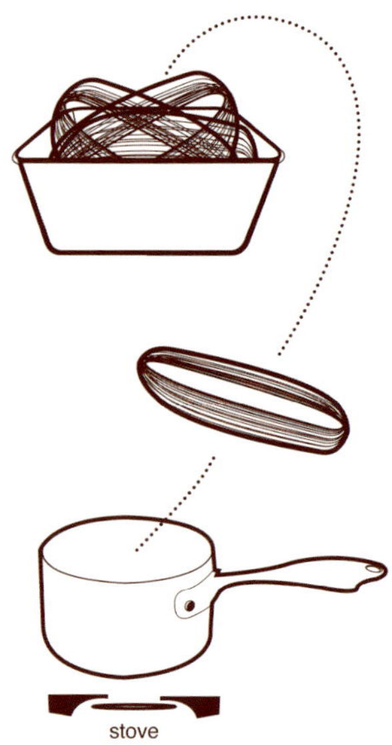

04.

rinsing and drying

Once dyed, all yarn must be given a quick rinse before drying.

Then you can start knitting!

chapter five

mixing colours

Dyes can be bought and used just as they are, straight from the pot. But the really exciting thing about dyeing your own yarn is the ability to mix your own colours. We have touched on this a little in chapter 03 but in this chapter I want to look at dyeing yarn in solid colours.

To dye yarn in one solid colour, you must use the immersion technique and also ensure that you have sufficient liquid to allow the yarn to move and dye evenly. For perfect results, you need 10 litres per 100 grams of dry-weight yarn. This means that in a normal domestic situation the most you can dye at any one time is 100 grams of yarn and, for the purposes of this book, I am assuming you are working in a normal domestic situation - i.e. your kitchen!

'But I want to dye enough yarn for a sweater,' I hear you cry. Well here are your options:

• cram all the yarn into the 10 litres of dye solution. Results will be all the same colour but with lots of shades.

• mix up the right amount of dye, then dye each 100-gram hank separately with 100ml of mixed dye. Results can be good but I find each hank is ever so slightly different. I don't like this as it looks like I have tried and failed.

• mix up 100ml of dyeing solution using 2 or 3 selected colours. Vary the mixture for each hank. The result will be hanks that are different colours but, because they have come from the same family of dyes, they will all 'go' together beautifully.

This is the method I will now explain in more detail.

you will need

01. Dye powder
02. Measuring spoons
03. Glass jars and spoons for mixing
04. Boiling water
05. Yarn
06. White vinegar or citric acid solution if not using the All-in-one acid dye
07. A bowl for soaking
08. 10-litre pan (not aluminium, as this affects the dye - stainless steel is best)
A smaller pan can be used but the yarn will not be dyed quite so evenly.

preparing the yarn

Wind five 100-gram hanks. Your yarn may well have arrived like this already in hanks.

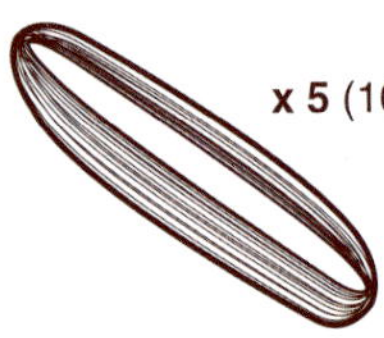

x 5 (100g) hanks

Secure the hanks in 4-5 places with a figure of eight knot. I try and use acrylic yarn for this as it is then easy to spot after the hank is dyed (acrylic yarn will not take the dye)
The yarn must then be soaked.

preparing the dye solution

For this type of dyeing you will need to make up 2 or 3 different colours.
For 500 grams of yarn (dry weight) make up two jars with 250ml of dye solution in each jar. Make up 50ml of a third colour to be used as shading if required.

250ml **250ml** **50ml**

01. 

02. 

03. 

04. 

05. 

06. 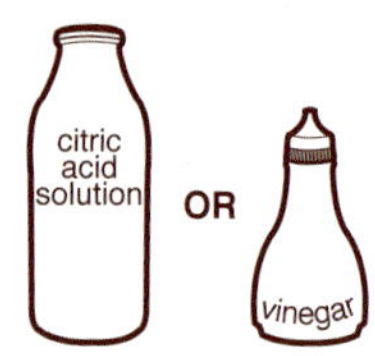

07. 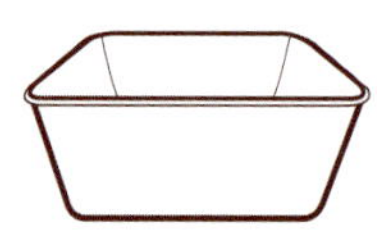

08. 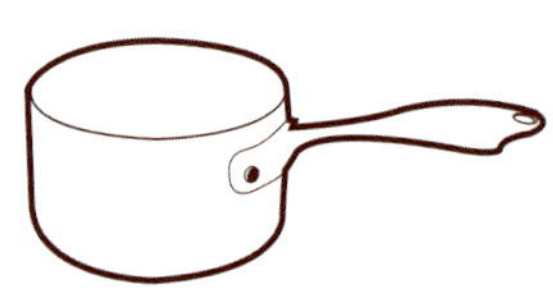

TIP
Always take care when handling dye powder.

TIP

You can test the colour you have mixed before dyeing the whole hank. Take about 1 metre (1 yard) of yarn, soak it, then put it in a little dish or on a piece of cling film. Add a couple of drops of the dye mixture. Squeeze the yarn to spread the dye. Cover and microwave for about 30 seconds on medium heat.

This will give you some idea of what the colour will look like. If you don't like it, you can mix in a bit more dye and test again.

Continue doing this until you achieve the colour you want. This is such fun and can be quite addictive - BEWARE!

the dyeing process

Each 100-gram hank is going to be dyed separately.

Put about 8 -10 litres of warm water into a pan. The more water you have, the more evenly dyed your yarn will be. If you don't mind a few variations to the colour, you can manage with less water.

mixing colours

Take another clean jar and to this jar add 10 dessertspoons of dye solution. (100ml in total)

This is when you can mix the colours. You can follow a system or just go wild - it's up to you.

SIMPLE SYSTEM
Decide which is your dominant colour (the one you like best) and use this as colour A. The shading colour is colour C and is optional.

	colour A	colour B	colour C
Hank 1	9 spoons	1 spoon	1 spoon
Hank 2	8 spoons	2 spoons	1 spoon
Hank 3	6 spoons	4 spoons	1 spoon
Hank 4	4 spoons	6 spoons	0 spoon
Hank 5	2 spoons	8 spoons	0 spoon

01.When you are happy with the colour, add the dye solution to the pan and stir.
02. Remove one hank from the soaking bowl.
03. Gently put it in the pan of warm dye water.
04. Stir, very gently, too much agitation can cause felting, just make sure all parts of the hank have absorbed the dye equally.

Bring the pan slowly up to temperature. The exact temperature required is 80° centigrade. But if you don't have a thermometer, don't worry, this is just below boiling point. Steam will be rising, the pan will be singing but no big bubbles have appeared. Keep at this temperature for 30 - 40 minutes.

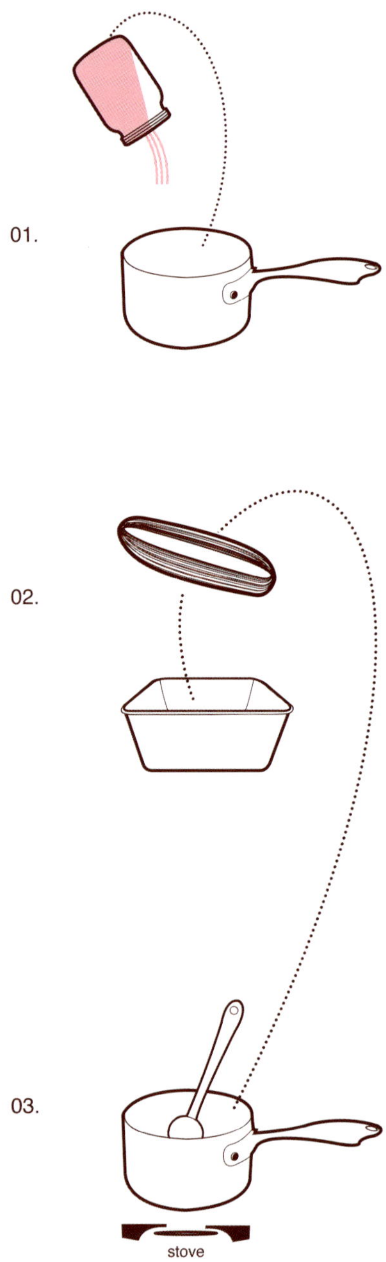

TIP

Don't worry if the temperature goes up and down a little - just DON'T let it boil. If it looks as though it is nearing boiling point - that is the bubbles rising are getting bigger and the singing is getting louder - remove the pot from the heat source and allow to cool down a bit. Turn the heat source down a little and after about 5 minutes, return the pot to the heat.

When the 30 - 40 minutes is up, take the pot off the heat. The water should now be clear or very pale. If it isn't, all is not lost! Put the pan back on the heat and add a couple of tablespoons of either white vinegar or citric acid solution to the pot. Heat up to dyeing point again and leave for 10 minutes. This should help with the total exhaustion of the dye.

Allow the pan and contents to cool.

rinsing and drying

Once dyed, all yarn must be given a quick rinse before drying.

SEE FRONT FLAP FOR MORE DETAILS

Dye the other 4 hanks in the same way, varying the colours.
The wonderful thing about this technique is that, because each colour you have mixed has come from the same 'family' of colours, they will naturally all blend together beautifully.

mixed with lemon yellow, turquoise, cerise and charcoal

cerise and slate

stone and sage

turquoise and lemon yellow

winter red and summer green

chapter six

01. 

02. 

03. 

04. 

05. 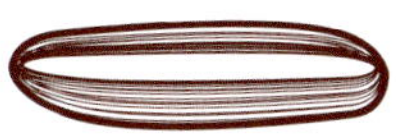

06. 

07. 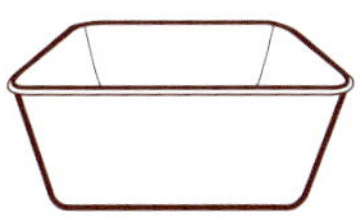

08. 

OR

09. 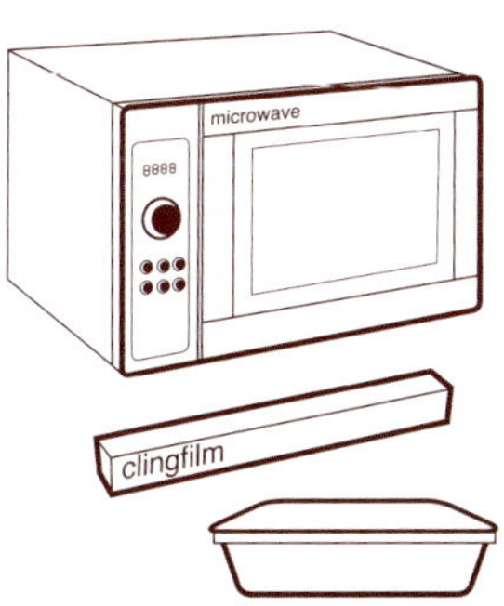

making stripes

Making striped yarn is great fun and amazingly easy. Once the yarn is dyed, the knitting is simple and the finished pieces look really clever! This chapter is all about making stripes in the microwave but don't forget you can also make stripes using the immersion technique – have a look at chapter 3 for more details

you will need

01. Dye powder
02. Measuring spoons
03. A glass jar and a spoon for mixing
04. Boiling water
05. 100 grams of yarn
(protein fibres or nylon)
06. White vinegar or citric acid solution if not using 'All-in-one' acid dyes
07. A bowl for soaking
08. A steamer and "boil-in-a-bag" plastic bags
OR
09. A microwave oven and a dish with a lid
(cling film can be used in place of a lid)

preparing the dye solution

Remember, if you are only dyeing half the hank in order to make a stripe, you will use less dye solution. For example, when dyeing half of a 100 gram hank, mix up 50ml of dye solution.

TIP
Always take care when handling dye powder.

preparing the yarn

The yarn must be wound into a long hank in order that you can knit at least three rows of the same colour.
To find the correct measurements for your project, you must do the following:
Using the same yarn and needles as for the project, cast on the correct number of stitches for one row / round.
Work five rows / rounds.
Mark the end of the yarn - the bit next to the last stitch knitted. Marking can be done with a pin, a knot, a clip or a piece of coloured yarn, whatever you have to hand.
Rip out three rows and measure the length of yarn that was used.
That is the size your hank needs to be when measured from end to end.

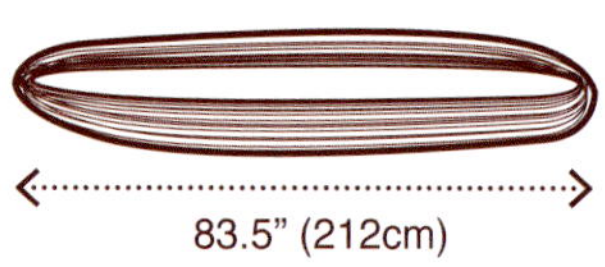

TIP

As you wind the yarn, the chairs are inclined to move towards each other so I put 4 hardback books between them on the table, and this keeps them in place.

The length of the hank will be half of the circumference.

Now if you don't want to bother with all that, I have done some calculations for you.
For socks knitted in the round on 60 stitches using 2.5 mm needles and using a fine sock wool, I make a hank that measures 83.5" (212 cm). (For the sock pattern, go to page 74.)

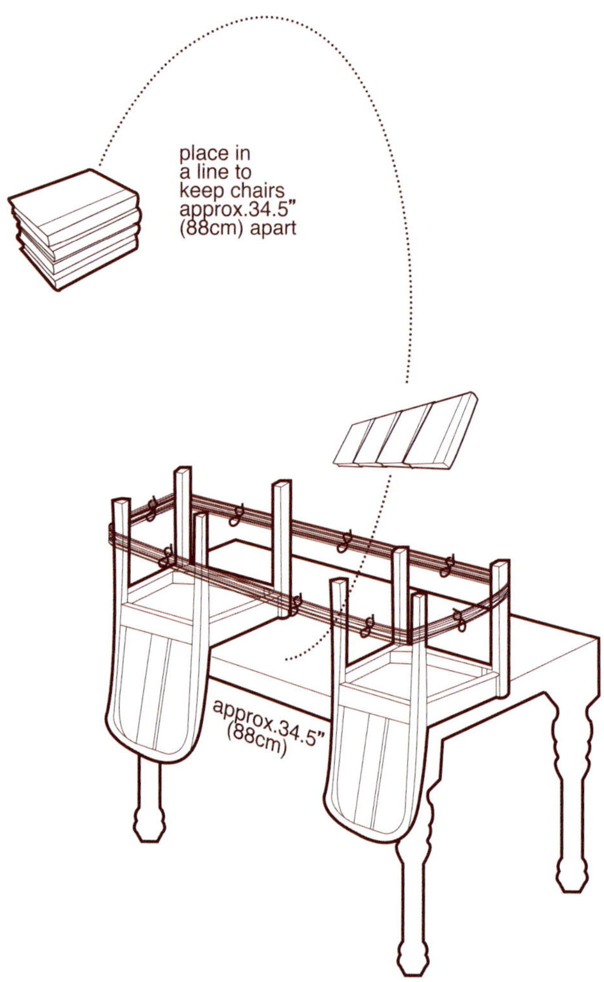

The hank can be easily wound by up-ending two chairs on a table. Have the chairs 34.5 in (88 cm) apart. This makes a hank about 83.5 in (212cm) long, perfect for a three-row stripe.

Once wound, secure the hank in 8 places with a figure-of-eight knot. I try and use acrylic yarn for this as it is then easy to spot after the hank is dyed (acrylic yarn will not take the dye).

The yarn must then be soaked.

the dyeing process

USING A MICROWAVE OVEN

01. Remove the yarn from the soaking bowl and place half (still dripping) in a suitable dish.

02. Put the other half, also dripping, in a good quality plastic bag. This is the half that won't be dyed.

03. Add 50ml of dye solution to the part of the hank in the dish. Gently move and squeeze the yarn to help the dye get to all parts - try not to leave any white bits, unless, of course, that is the effect you are after. If you can't get rid of the white bits, just add a little more dye solution.

04. Cover the dish with a lid, tuck the end of the plastic bag inside the dish, then put the bag on top of the lid. This ensures that all the fibre is covered.

05. Place in the microwave for 10 minutes on medium heat. Check after 5 minutes to make sure no yarn is drying out. If it is, turn the hank until it is all wet again. Be careful as the fibres and liquid will be very hot. Return to the microwave for the final 5 minutes.

Take the dish out of the oven and carefully remove the lid. Check the residue liquid. This should be clear or pale by now. If it is still quite dark, replace the lid as before and 'cook' for another 5 minutes on medium heat.

06. Leave to cool completely. Any dye that is left in the residue liquid will be absorbed during this time.

01.

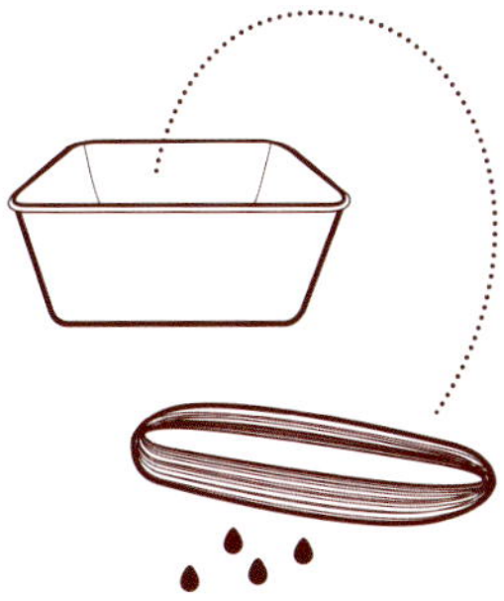

02.

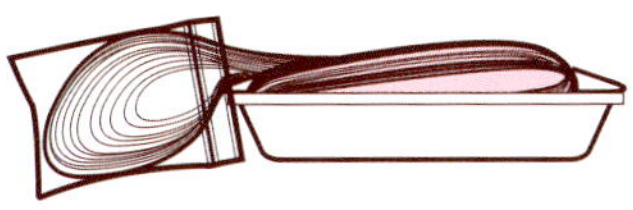

03.

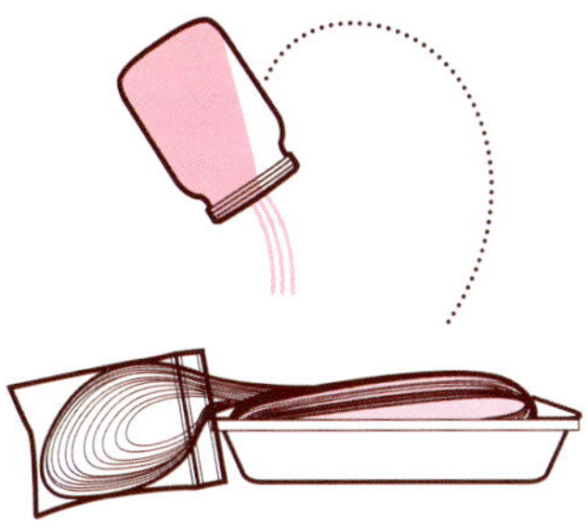

04.

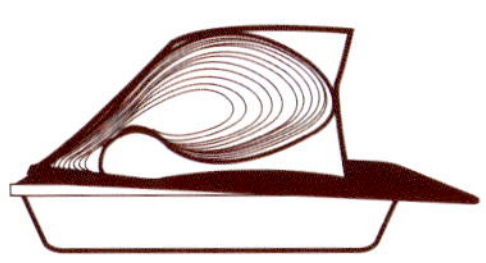

05.

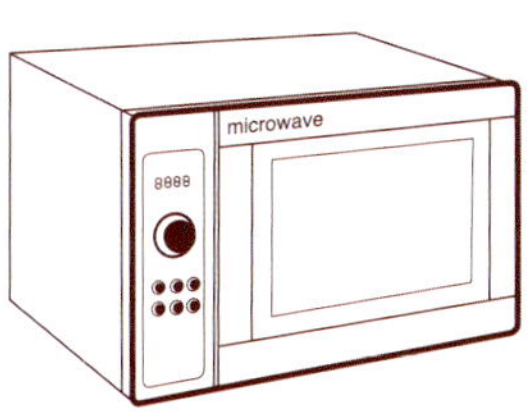

06.

USING A STEAMER

01. Remove the hank from the soaking bowl and place half in one good quality plastic bag, ('boil-in-a-bag' bags are excellent) and the other half in another bag.

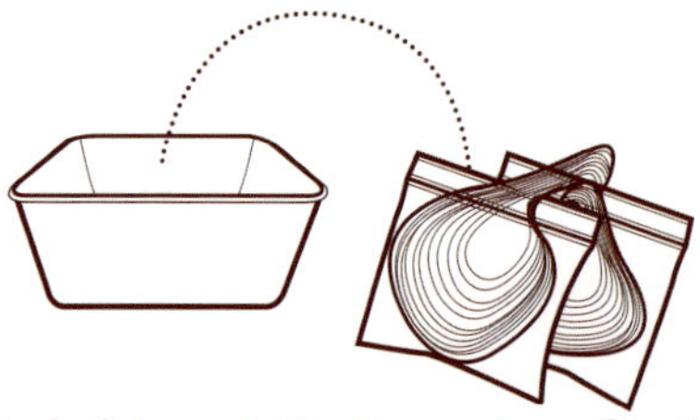

02. Add 50ml of dye solution to one bag. Gently move and squeeze the yarn to help the dye get to all parts, try not to leave any white bits, unless, of course, that is the effect you are after. If you can't get rid of the white bits, just add a bit more dye.

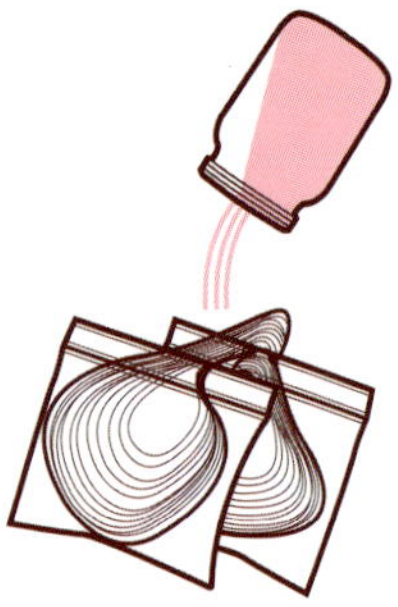

03. Place the two bags in a steamer or in a colander over a pan of boiling water. Put them side by side with the openings at the top.

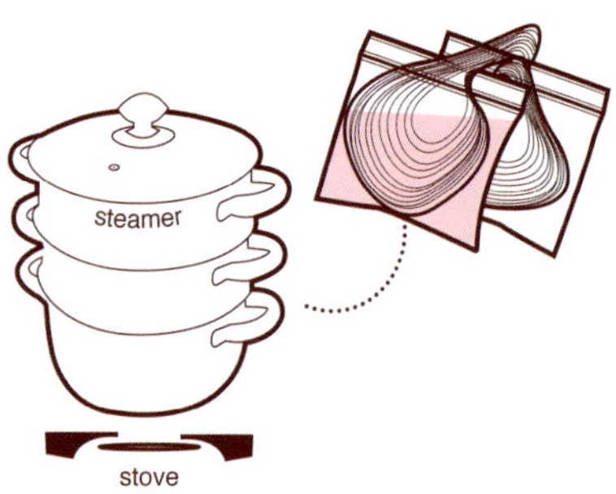

04. Cover the pan with a lid and steam for 30 - 40 minutes.

05. Leave to cool.

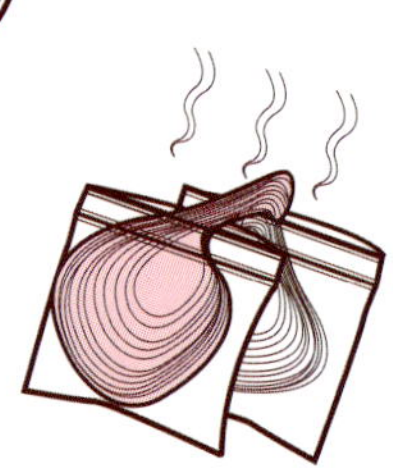

rinsing and drying

Once dyed, all yarn must be given a quick rinse before drying.

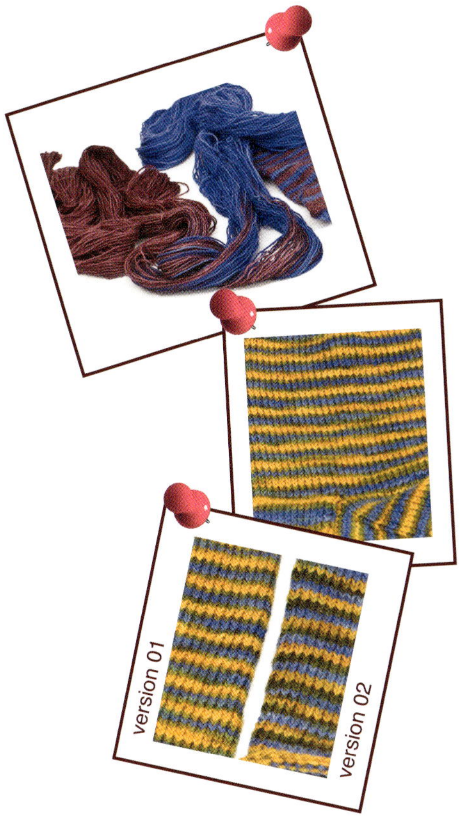

variations

1. TWO COLOURS

Once you have dyed one half of the hank one colour and finished the rinsing stage, you can then repeat the whole operation, dyeing the other half in a different colour.

2. THREE COLOURS, **VERSION ONE**

Make up the hank and the dye solutions as before. Now, instead of dyeing half the hank in the first colour, dye two thirds of the hank in the first colour, leaving just one third undyed.

After the rinsing stage, take the hank and dye two thirds of the hank in the second colour, leaving just one third the first colour. Where the two colours overlap will give you the third colour. You will end up with 2 main stripes edged with a mixed colour. This softens the effect of the stripes and I think looks rather good.

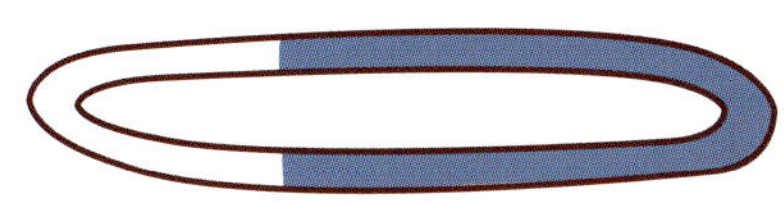

first dye blue

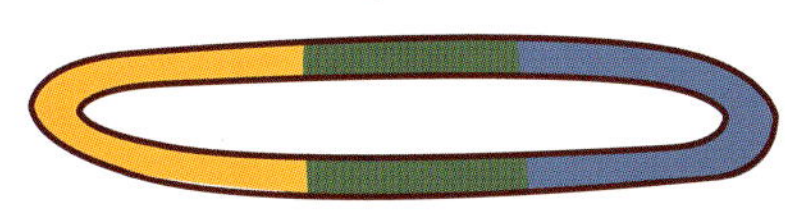

second dye yellow, overlap creates the green

3. THREE COLOURS, **VERSION TWO**

In this variation you end up with three separate stripes.

Make up the hank and the dye solutions as before. Now, instead of dyeing half the hank in the first colour, dye two thirds of the hank, leaving just one third undyed.
After the rinsing stage, take the hank, fold it as shown and dye two thirds of the hank in the second colour, leaving just one third the first colour. Where the two colours overlap will give you the third colour. Notice the different way the hank has been folded. This will give you three separate stripes. It all makes sense when you do it!

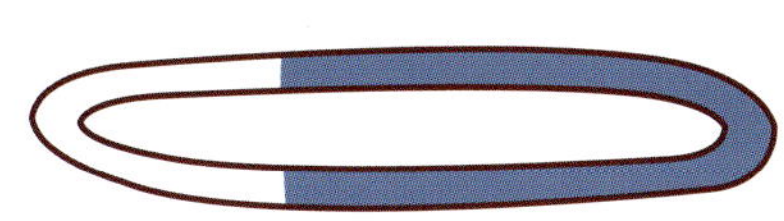

first dye blue

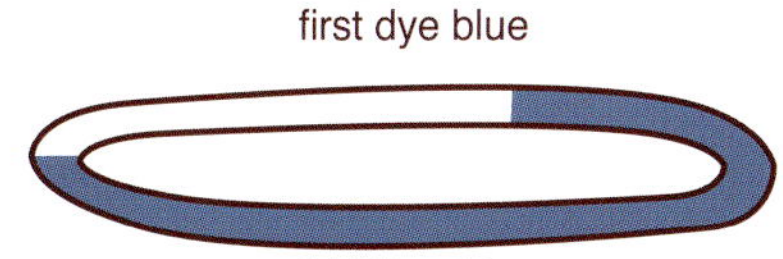

fold like this

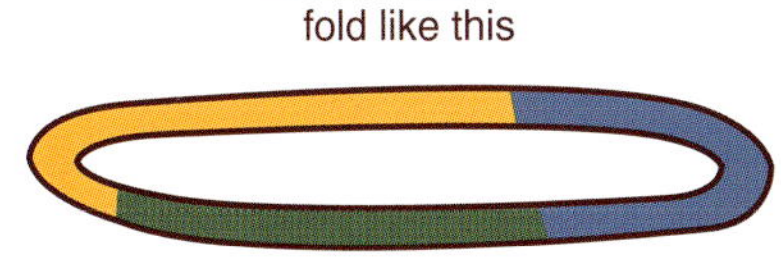

second dye yellow, (yellow goes over the blue to make the green)

chapter seven

01. 

02. 

03. 

04. 

05. 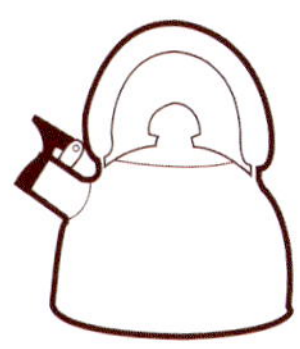

06. 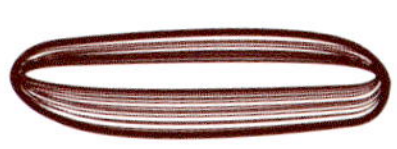

07. 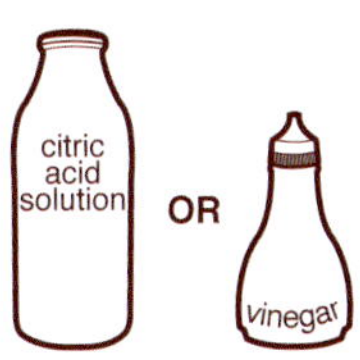

08. 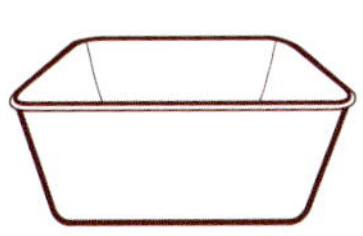

09. 

OR

10. 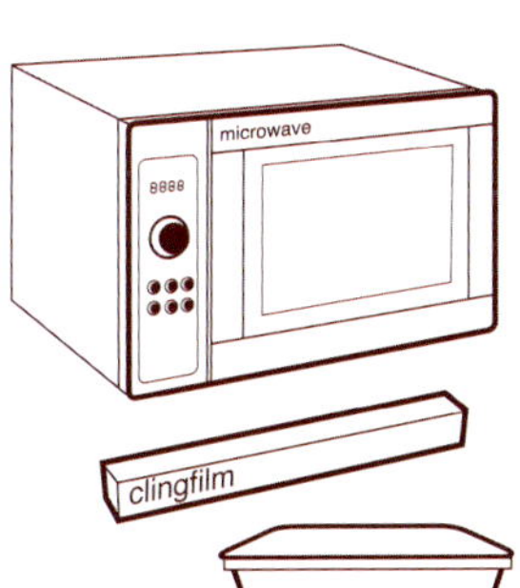

11. 

painting the yarn

Instead of pouring on dye solution, yarn can be painted using a thickened solution. This gives you more control but is more time consuming and can be a bit messy - or perhaps that's just me. (Use plastic gloves when doing this technique.)

you will need

01. Dye powder
02. Manutex (Sodium alginate) see suppliers list on page 96
03. Measuring spoons
04. A glass jar and spoon for mixing
05. Boiling water
06. 100 grams of yarn (protein fibres or nylon)
07. White vinegar or citric acid solution if not using 'All-in-one' acid dyes
08. Bowl for soaking
09. A steamer and "boil-in-a-bag" plastic bags
OR
10. A microwave oven and a dish with a lid (cling film can be used in place of a lid)
11. Plastic clips - the sort that are sold for keeping bags closed and airtight.

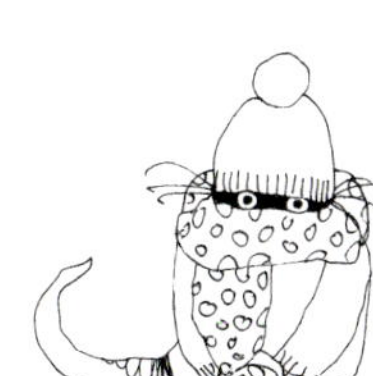

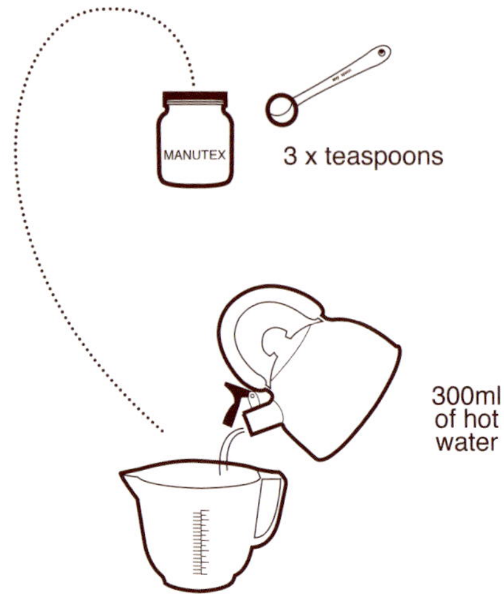

getting ready

MAKING THE BASIC DYE PASTE

Manutex (sodium alginate) is available from good dye suppliers. There are other thickening agents but I find this the easiest to use. It looks a bit like brown sugar but is a seaweed extract. The best thing is to make a batch of paste and keep what you don't use in a jar with a lid in the fridge - well labelled of course.
This will keep for a couple of weeks.

Dissolve 3 teaspoons of manutex in 300ml of water.

Do this by sprinkling the granules on top of very hot water, stirring briskly at the same time.

To prevent lumps forming, keep stirring for 3 minutes or so continuously, and then every now and then until the mixture has cooled.
By the time the mixture has cooled, it has the consistency of runny honey. This paste is then made into dye paste by adding dye powder.

SAFETY TIPS

As a powder, the dye can be a hazard because it is so fine and can, very easily, become air-borne and then inhaled. A few sensible pre-cautions at this stage can avoid problems!

01. Mix up the dye before you start and then put away the remaining dye powder, out of harm's way.
02. Make sure there is not a draught – e.g. don't use dye powder by an open window.
03. Wear a mask – particularly if you are prone to asthma.

Different amounts of dye powder are needed for different types of dye. Follow the recipes below for a good medium colour. Use more powder for a stronger shade and less for a paler shade.

basic acid dye

½ teaspoon to 100ml paste

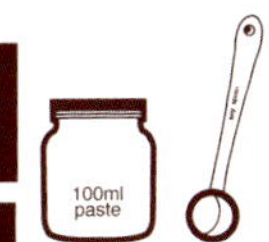

½ x teaspoon

procion fibre-reactive dye

1 teaspoon to 100ml paste

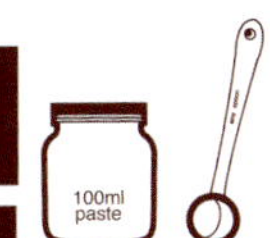

1 x teaspoon

all-in-one acid dye

1 ½ teaspoon of dye to 100ml paste

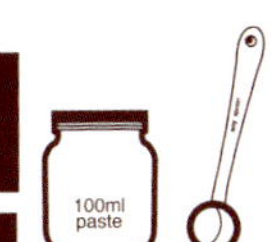

1 ½ x teaspoon

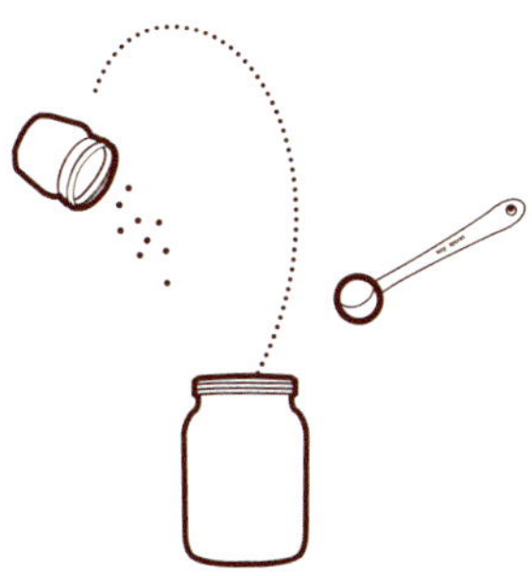

Put 100ml of paste into a separate container. Sprinkle on the dye powder and mix thoroughly. This paste will keep for a couple of weeks if covered and kept in the fridge. Remember to label it well!

preparing the yarn

Wind the yarn into a hank, if it has come as a ball. Secure the hank in 4-5 places with a figure-of-eight knot.

I try and use acrylic yarn for this as it is then easy to spot after the hank is dyed (acrylic yarn will not take the dye)

In order to mark the different areas of the hank to be painted, I find it quite useful to attach clips to the hank before it is soaked.
The clips also make it easier to hold the yarn while it is being painted.

The yarn must then be soaked.

painting the yarn

Gently take the hank from the soaking bowl and squeeze to remove excess liquid.

01. Lay out a piece of cling film on a flat surface. Arrange the section of yarn you want to paint on top of the cling film. Place a clip at each end of this section. I find the clips make the yarn easier to handle while painting.

Spread the yarn to expose as many strands as possible.

02. The paste is then applied with a brush. I prefer the foam brushes for this.

03. When you have applied the paste to one side, place a second piece of cling film on top of the painted section. Smooth this out so it is sticking to the painted area.

Variations

SPOTS

Make a long hank - as for making the striped yarn on page 38.

Paint half the hank one solid colour and paint the other half in stripes, each stripe being about one inch (2.5cm) wide. When knitted, this will come out as spots.

When you are knitting, try and line up the coloured stitches.

SPIRAL PATTERN

I've painted these sections in stripes (twirl)

This is for a fine sock yarn knitted on 2.5mm needles with 60 stitches in the round.
Make a hank 27 in (69cm) in length.
Place six clips 9 in (23cm) apart.
Paint both section As one colour, paint both section Bs the second colour and both section Cs the third colour.

Oops, a tension change

Things that can happen while you are knitting. Depending on your tension, the spirals can go either clockwise or anti-clockwise (it doesn't really matter) but if your tension changes mid-sock, you might find yourself going in the other direction! Still looks good though.

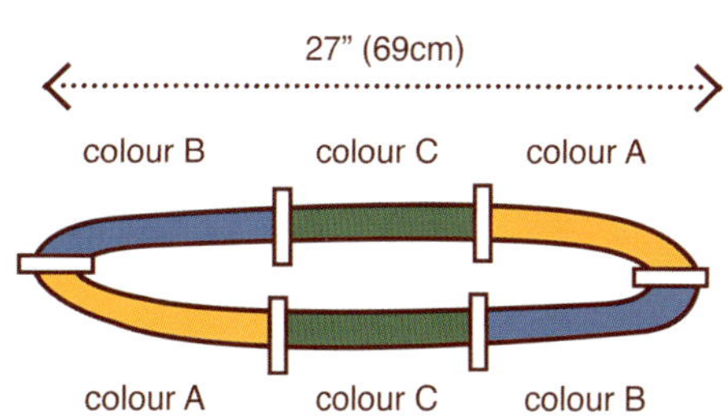

Chapter eight

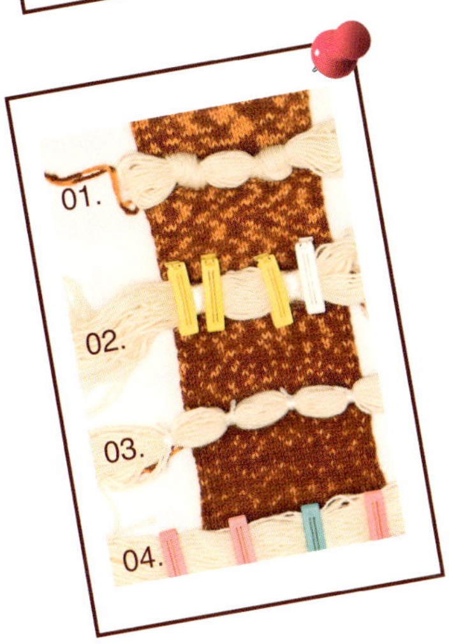

tie and dye

Many of you will be familiar with tie-and-dye techniques on fabric. This is when pieces of cloth are tied up in different ways, then dyed. The dye cannot penetrate to these tied areas, so creating beautiful patterns.

This same technique can be applied to yarn and although actual patterns are not created, the resulting yarn can be very interesting, particularly when it has been knitted.

tying the yarn

There are 4 basic ways of tying yarn. Whichever method you choose, the yarn must first be wound into a hank.

01. Knots – easy to do but hard to undo!
Knots are tied at intervals along the hank. This creates quite large areas that are randomly dyed.

02. Clips and cling film – quick and easy to undo. First wrap about an inch of the hank with cling film – not too tightly. Then attach clips either side of this area, making sure you clip over the cling film.

This creates slightly larger areas of undyed yarn. A bit of dye might creep in, but this is a lot easier than all that binding.

03. Binding – time consuming to do and undo.
Using another piece of yarn bind, certain areas of the hank, very tightly. I like to use acrylic or cotton yarn for this as it is easier to spot after dyeing.
This gives very defined areas of undyed yarn, the size of which can be varied by the amount of binding.

04. Clips – very quick and easy to undo. Clips can be used on the hank. These give very small areas of undyed yarn, about the amount needed for one stitch.

dyeing the yarn

Yarn can be dyed using either the immersion method or the microwave.
I do find that less dye penetrates under the tied or clipped areas if the immersion technique is used. This means that the undyed areas are larger.

If dyeing with this method, please refer to chapter 3 as the technique is exactly the same once the hank has been tied, bound or clipped.
If, however, you want smaller more defined areas undyed, then the microwave technique seems to be better.

dyeing in the microwave

I have explained this here as the method is slightly different from the method described in chapter 2.

YOU WILL NEED

01. Dye powder
02. Measuring spoons
03. A glass jar and spoon for mixing
04. Boiling water
05. 100 grams of yarn (protein fibres or nylon)
06. White vinegar or citric acid solution if not using 'All-in-one' acid dyes
07. Bowl for soaking
08. Microwave oven
09. 2 litre jug

01.

02.

03.

04.

05.

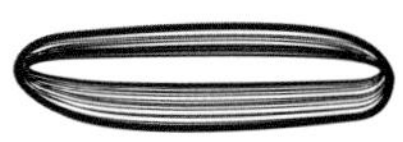

06.

07.

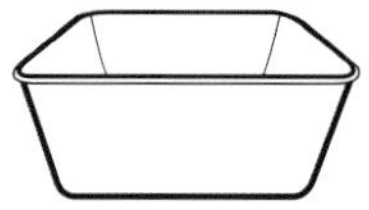

08.

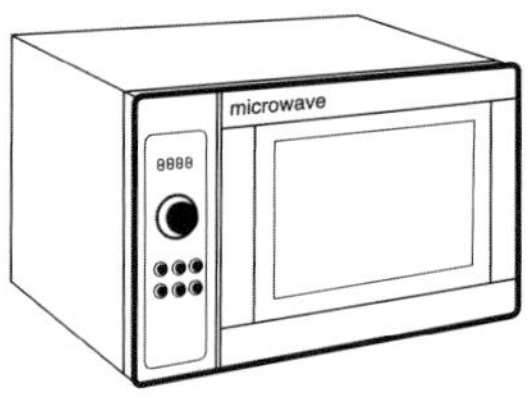

09.

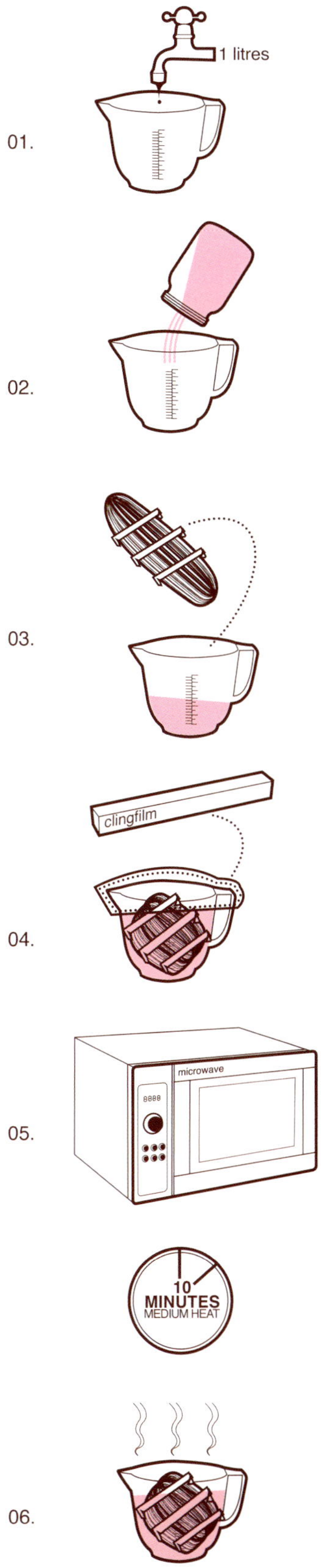

preparing the dye solution

preparing the yarn

Wind the yarn into a hank, if it has come as a ball. Secure the hank in 4-5 places with a figure of eight knot. I try and use acrylic yarn for this as it is then easy to spot after the hank is dyed. (acrylic yarn will not take the dye)
Clip, tie or bind the hank either before or after soaking as this seems to make little difference. The yarn must then be soaked.

the dyeing process

01. Put I litre of water in a 2 litre jug or bowl.
02. Add 100mls of dye solution.
03. Add the soaked and tied yarn. Turn it round a little to make sure the dye is distributed evenly throughout the yarn.
04. Cover with cling film. Pierce a few holes in the cling film with a pin.
05. Microwave on medium heat for 10 minutes.
06. Allow to cool before rinsing.

rinsing and drying

All yarn, once dyed must first be given a quick rinse before drying.

It's then time to start knitting
– Hurray!

ideas to try

TWO COLOURS
To get two different colours, yarn can be prepared in different ways:

01. It can be dyed in the first colour, then tied up and dyed in the second colour.

02. It can be tied up, dyed in the first colour, untied and dyed in the second colour.
It doesn't really matter which way round you do it. Just remember, if you are dyeing with a light colour, you will get a more defined pattern if you dye the light colour when the hank is untied.

03. A third option is to start with coloured yarn - perhaps something you bought and you now don't like. In this case, the yarn is tied up and then dyed just once in another colour.

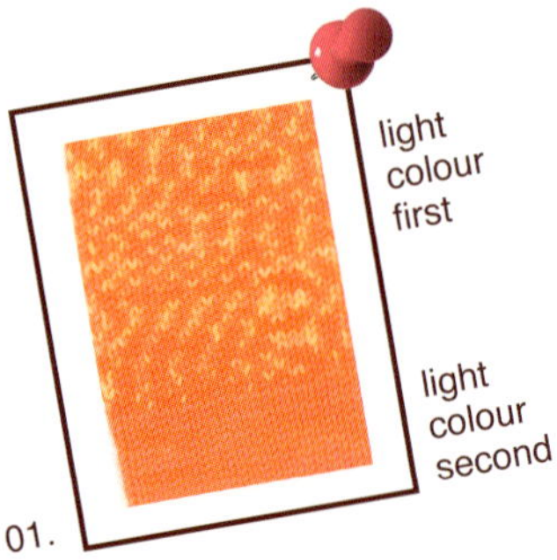

01.

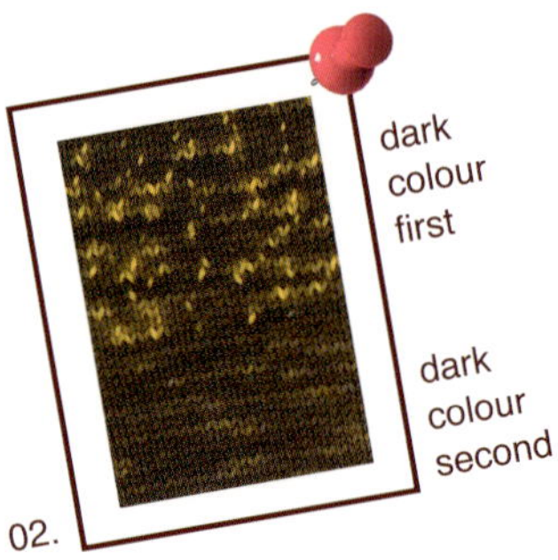

02.

03.

THE TWEED EFFECT
This has got to be one of my favourite ways of dyeing. It is such fun and the results can be startling.
It is just a matter of clipping and dyeing, then unclipping, re-clipping and dyeing some more.
Here's how it works.
Wind the yarn into a hank that measures about 1 metre (39 inches)from end to end.
Make up three solutions of dye. I like to use the three primary colours, that is cerise, turquoise and lemon.
To dye a 100-gram hank, you will need 100ml of each colour. This gives a really strong colour; use less if you would prefer a softer shade.
You are going to dye some yarn that is basically brown with flashes of turquoise, purple, green, yellow, orange and cerise.
The flashes will come at about 3-inch intervals. This means that clips are put on the hank at about 3-inch intervals. The trick comes when some of the clips are left off!

THE TWEED EFFECT

01. Begin by placing 6 clips on the hank as shown. The dotted marks are where clips will be going later.

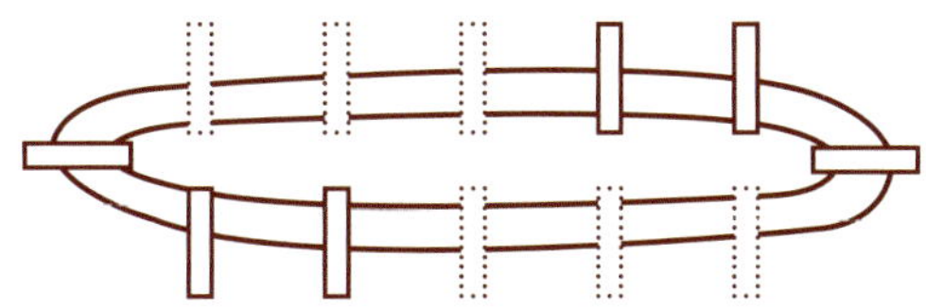

02. Dye in yellow.

03. Take off 4 clips to reveal 4 white stripes. Replace the clips as shown.

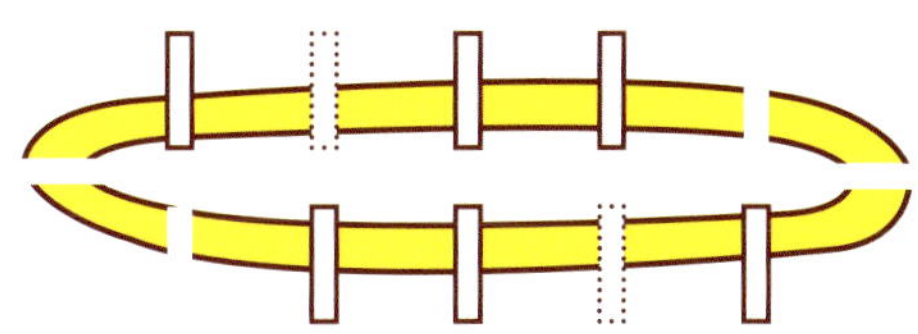

04. Dye in turquoise.

05. Take off 4 clips to reveal 2 white and 2 yellow stripes. Replace as shown.

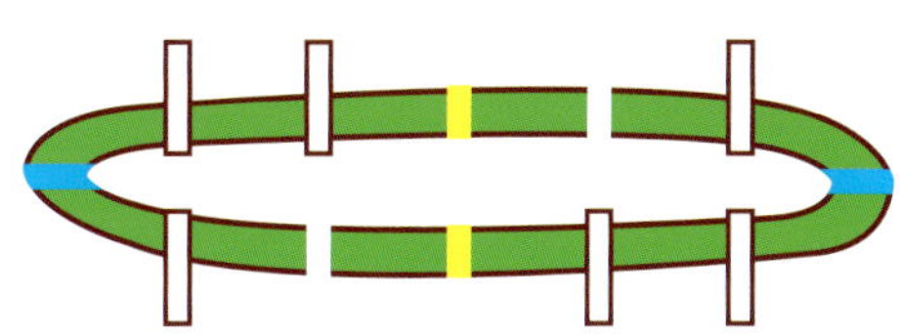

06. Dye in cerise.

07. Remove all clips and WOW! You should have stripes in purple, turquoise, cerise, orange, green and yellow.

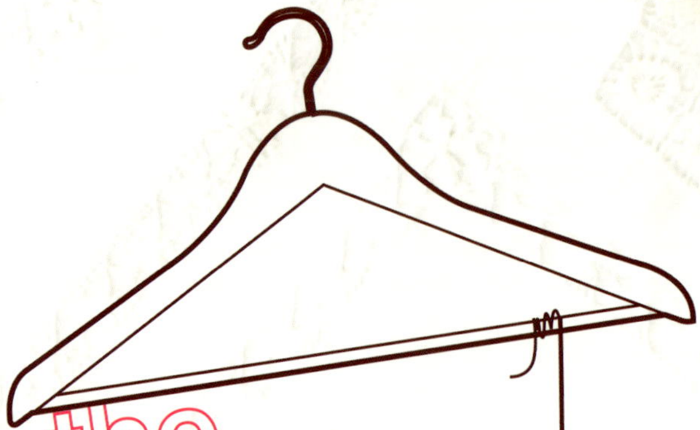

the patterns

chapter nine

Balls of difficulty

In your sleep

A sinch

Tricky

Fiendish

fair isle bag

This pattern is a lovely example of the benefits of creating a colour family as described in Chapter 5. The starting point was three wildly different colours. Used neat, they don't look great together. But by mixing them using varying quantities of each colour, a family is created. When then used in a pattern like this, the result can be quite magical! This bag lends itself extremely well to a knitting project bag, but can of course also be used as a trendy handbag. It is lined and you can either go for a fabric in complementary colours (if you buy some natural coloured silk, you can dye it with the same dyes as the yarn for the bag, using the same basic microwave method). Alternatively, you can opt to contrast the colour(s) of the lining fabric. Whatever you choose, do make sure that the lining fabric has a fairly dense weave, especially if you want to carry your knitting in it, so your needles won't poke through the fabric and out of your bag.

about this pattern

difficulty

size

The base of the bag measures 34 x 11 cm (13 x 4 in) and tapers a little to approx. 25 x 11 cm (10 x 4 in). The height is 21 cm (8 in) at the striped edges and 28 cm (11 in) from base to handles.

materials

approx. 150 grams Tall Yarns Superwash Bamboo sock yarn (80% merino, 20% bamboo; 400 m per 100 grams) or equivalent 4-ply yarn

metreage needed

Approx. 600 m

tension

28 sts and 31 rows measure 10 x 10 cm (4 x 4 in) in Stocking Stitch Fair Isle*

notions

one pair of 3.25 mm needles (or bigger or smaller to help you achieve gauge)
one pair of thick, strong needles, 6.5 – 8 mm (for handles)

* When you knit Fair Isle, your gauge changes from what it would be when knitting st.st in one colour. To give you an example: when I knitted a gauge swatch in one colour of this same yarn, I achieved a gauge of 25 sts x 37 rows (measuring 10 x 10 cm/4 x 4 in). In Fair Isle, using the same yarn, it worked out at 28 x 31. So please do check carefully, unless you don't mind if your finished bag comes out a slightly different size.

stitches

stocking stitch: One row K, one row P
moss stitch: One st K, one st P. Start next row with the same st you finished with (i.e. if your last st was K, then start the next row with a K st) to ensure that you don't end up knitting a single rib.
I-cord: See "useful stitches" on page 94.

the pattern

fair isle panel (knit 2)

Cast on 91 sts.
Rows 1 – 20: Knit in st.st Fair Isle, starting with Chart 1 (see p.60)
Note: the bold lines on the charts show exactly one repeat of that particular motif. Notice that the motifs have different repeats, the smallest being 4 sts (ch. 5) and the biggest being 14 sts (ch. 2). Because of this, it does not exactly matter on which stitch you start a motif, as long as you work the charts from right to left and from row 1 up. This ensures that the pattern of your knitting follows the chart, which helps you spot any mistakes quickly and easily.
Row 21: S1, K2tog, K row 7 of the chart until 3 sts from end, SSK, K1 (89 sts).
Continue knitting the Fair Isle charts in sequence, decreasing 1 st at either side of every 4th row until you have 65 sts left on the needle. If you decrease on the correct rows, the last decrease is on row 21 of chart 4.
After the last decrease, continue knitting the last 2 charts without any further change in the number of stitches. Chart 5 is the only one starting on a P row (due to Chart 4 ending on a K row).
When knitting the last row of Chart 5, cast off the middle 37 sts. Finish the row. Put the 14 remaining sts on each side on a stitch holder or a scrap piece of wool.

striped gusset (knit 1)

Cast on 30 sts in Col 1.
Row 1: K
Row 2: K1, P1 to end of row
Row 3: change to Col 2, K1, P1 to end of row
Row 4: change to Col 3, K1, P1 to end of row
Row 5: change to Col 4, K1, P1 to end of row
Row 6: change to Col 5, K1, P1 to end of row
Row 7: change to Col 6, K1, P1 to end of row
Row 8: change to Col 7, K1, P1 to end of row
Row 9: change to Col 1, K1, P1 to end of row

Repeat rows 3 – 9 until the total length of the gusset is long enough to reach from the top of Chart 4 on one of your Fair Isle panels, around the bottom and up the other side to the same point (see picture of finished bag). This should measure approx. 78 cm (31 in). Finish on Col 1.
K one extra row in Col 1 and cast off all sts.

making up the bag

i-cord

Knit an i-cord (see page 95) that is long enough to run along all 4 edges of the gusset (approx. 178 cm / 70 in).

block your knitting

Block the panels and the gusset by lightly steaming them on the medium heat setting of your iron. Check that you lightly stretch both of your panels into the same size and shape when they are back to back on top of each other.

TIP
To avoid your needle handles ever getting pulled out of the bag, fix them by dropping a couple of small drops of superglue in between the stitches on the needles and allow to dry.

cutting the lining

This is the right time to cut the fabric for your lining to the right size. Re-measure your gusset and panels. Cut one piece of fabric the size of your gusset, and 2 pieces the size of your panels, allowing approx. 1 cm (1/3 in) seam allowance on all sides. If you want any extra pockets inside your bag, cut those as well.

handles

Put the stitches of one of your Fair Isle panels back on one of the needles so that you have the right side of the work facing you when you hold the needle in your left hand. Knit the first 14 sts using one of the big needles you have chosen as your handles. Push them back on the big needle to make space for the other 14 sts.
Repeat this process with the other panel, ensuring you pick up your stitches in the opposite direction and purling them, to ensure that both your big needles point in the same direction when you put your panels back to back (see picture of finished bag).

sewing the bag

Now pin one long side of the gusset along the edge of one of the panels, making sure that you don't stretch them and that the gusset reaches the same point on either side of the panel (roughly the top of Chart 4). Sew the two together using mattress stitch.
Repeat with the other panel along the opposite edge of the gusset. Make sure both of your panels are facing out.
Pin the i-cord along all edges of the gusset so that it neatly covers the seams. Where the i-cord runs along the short sides of the gusset, slightly gather the gusset so the i-cord helps to firm up the edge of the gusset.
On the sewing machine, sew your lining bag together and attach any inner pockets you are adding. Put the lining into the knitted bag so that the wrong side of the lining faces the wrong side of the knitting.

Fold in the seam allowances of the edges of the fabric and pin them along the edges of the knitted bag. Sew the lining into the bag, either by hand or on the sewing machine (the lining of the bag in the picture was sewn on the machine; this gives slightly more structure to the bag). Step back and admire your work.

dyeing recipes

Start with two 100 grams hanks, wind the first hank into 4 hanks of 25 grams each. Wind 2 additional 25 grams hanks from the second hank. Tie them all with figure of eights as explained in Chapter 5. Leave the remaining 50 grams un-dyed.
Dye the six 25 grams hanks as follows:
1. 8 TBS Pale Pumpkin, 2 drops of Winter Red ("pumpkin")
2. 5 TBS Slate ("blue")
3. 2 TBS Winter Red, 2 TBS Slate ("maroon")
4. 1 TBS Red, 4 TBS Slate ("purple")
5. 4 TBS Pale Pumpkin, 1.5 TBS Slate ("lilac")
6. 4 TBS Red, 1 TSP Slate, 1 TSP Pumpkin ("red")

Microwave time: 4 mins per hank on MEDIUM
Once dyed and dry, wind all hanks into little balls, incl. the un-dyed yarn ("cream").

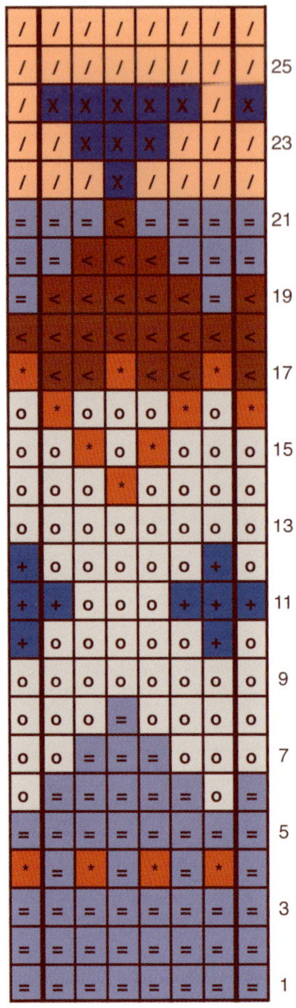

Chart 1

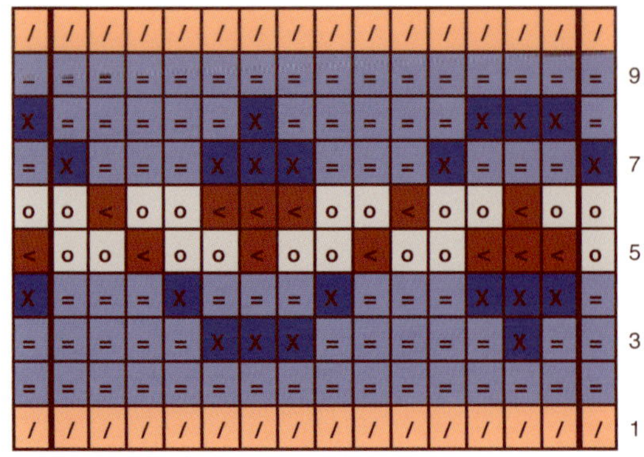

Chart 2

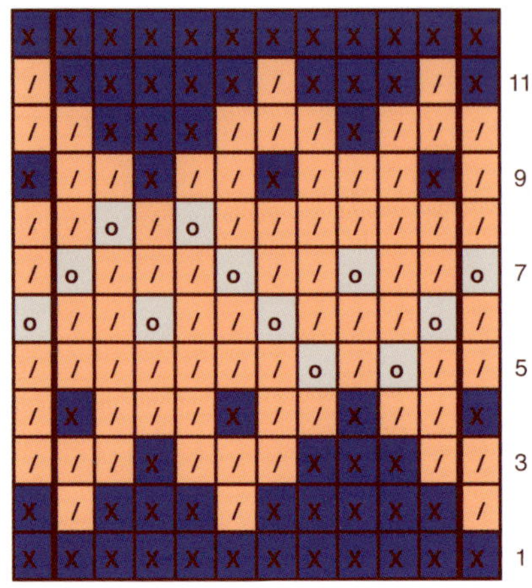

Chart 3

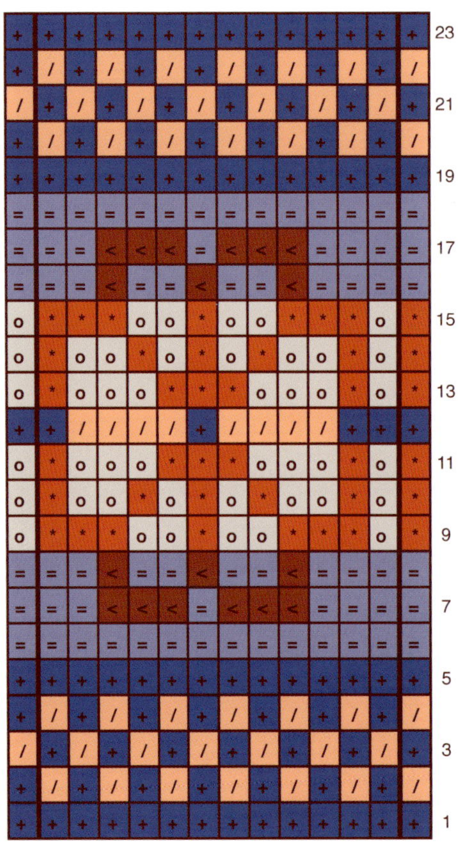

Chart 4

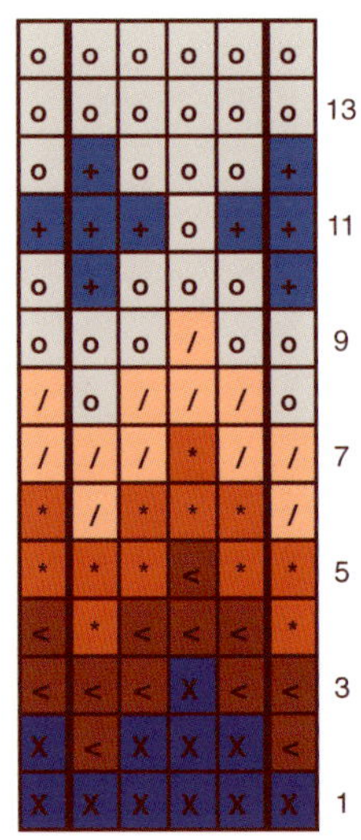

Chart 5

=	Lilac	<	Maroon
*	Red	X	Purple
o	Cream	/	Pumpkin
+	Blue		

groovy beret

This pattern allows for some flexibility of yarn, needles and gauge. The hat is knitted in a repeat of panels that are knitted in sequence. Since it is knitted around the head instead of top-down (or bottom-up), you can adapt the number of repeats of the panel to fit your head.

The pattern lends itself extremely well to self-patterning yarn or home-dyed two-tone yarn since these create vertical stripes, giving the hat an unusual look and emphasising the direction of the knitting. A similar effect can be achieved by knitting with 2 colours and changing colour every couple of rows. For a child-size version, cast on the smaller number of stitches (48) and knit the right number of repeats to fit the head, just like the adult 56-stitch size.

about this pattern

difficulty

measurements
Each panel adds approx. 5 cm (2 in) to the head circumference

materials
Tall Yarns DK (225 metres per 100 grams) or equivalent double knitting yarn. One hank will be enough, even for a big head!

metreage needed
Approx. 20 metres per panel. 8 - 10 panels for a grown-up size hat.

tension
20 sts and 26 rows measure 10 x 10 cm

notions
One pair of 4.5 mm needles
One cable needle of a similar diameter

stitches

stocking stitch: One row K, one row P

thepattern

Cast on 48 (56) sts loosely
Row 1: (WS) S1, P37 (45), K1, P6, K1, P2
Row 2: (RS) S1, K1, P1, K6, P1, K37 (45), W&T
Row 3: SWS, P37 (45), W&T
Row 4: SWS, K36 (44), W&T
Row 5: SWS, P36 (44), K1, P6, K1, P2
Row 6: S1, K1, P1, place 3 sts on a double pointed or cable needle, K next 3 sts, now K the 3 sts from the cable needle, P1, K35 (43), W&T
Row 7: SWS, P35 (43), K1, P6, K1, P2
Row 8: S1, K1, P1, K6, P1, K34 (42), W&T
Row 9: SWS, P34 (42), W&T
Row 10: SWS, K33 (41), W&T
Row 11: SWS, P33 (41), K1, P6, K1, P2
Row 12: S1, K1, P1, K6, P1, K32 (40), W&T
Row 13: SWS, P32 (40), K1, P6, K1, P2
Row 14: S1, K1, P1, place 3 sts on a double pointed or cable needle, K next 3 sts, now K the 3 sts from the cable needle, P1, K31 (39), W&T
Row 15: SWS, P31 (39), W&T
Row 16: SWS, K30 (38), W&T
Row 17: SWS, P30 (38), K1, P6, K1, P2
Row 18: S1, K1, P1, K6, P1, K38 (46) – picking up the wraps with each of the last 8 sts when knitting them

Repeat these 18 rows until you achieve the desired size.

When you're happy with the number of panels (as a guide, you'll need 8 panels for a smallish head and 10 for a large head), cast off all the stitches as you knit row 18. Leave a long (approx. 40 cm / 16 in) end, which you can use to sew the sides of the hat together.

finishing

With the long end of yarn and a darning needle, gather the stitches along the edge of the crown together and pull tight. Then sew along the cast-on and cast-off edges of the hat, taking care to line up the stitches as you go. Especially when you reach the ribbed edge of the hat, choose carefully where you join the 2 sides to ensure a nice continuation of the rib. Sew in the ends of yarn.

dyeing recipe

Follow the dyeing instructions for dyeing stripes, chapter 6. When winding the long hank, place the seats of the chairs you are winding the yarn around approx. 88 cm / 34.5 in apart on the table. When you dye half the hank at this length, you will achieve a similar stripy effect to the hat in the picture. The colours used for this hat were Sage and Pale Pumpkin. They were combined in a dish (and squidged together a lot) to create this blended, soft colour.

groovy beret

	56	55	54	53	52	51	50	49	48	47	46	45	44	43	42	41	40	39	38	37	36	35	34	33	32	31	30	29	28	27	26	25	24	23	22	21	20	19	18	17	16	15	14	13	12	11	10	9	8	7	6	5	4	3	2	1	
18	I	I	I	I	I	I	I	I	I	I	I	I	I	I	I	I	I	I	I	I	I	I	I	I	I	I	I	I	I	I	I	I	I	I	I	I	I	I	I	I	I	I	I	I	I	I	--	I	I	I	I	I	I	--	I	S	18
17								S	--	--	--	--	--	--	--	--	--	--	--	--	--	--	--	--	--	--	--	--	--	--	--	--	--	--	--	--	--	--	--	--	--	--	--	--	--	--	I	--	--	--	--	--	--	I	--	--	17
16								W	I	I	I	I	I	I	I	I	I	I	I	I	I	I	I	I	I	I	I	I	I	I	I	I	I	I	I	I	I	I	I	I	I	I	I	I	I	I	S										16
15							S	--	--	--	--	--	--	--	--	--	--	--	--	--	--	--	--	--	--	--	--	--	--	--	--	--	--	--	--	--	--	--	--	--	--	--	--	--	--	--	W										15
14							W	I	I	I	I	I	I	I	I	I	I	I	I	I	I	I	I	I	I	I	I	I	I	I	I	I	I	I	I	I	I	I	I	I	I	I	I	I	I	I	--	6	6	6	6	6	6	--	I	S	14
13						S	--	--	--	--	--	--	--	--	--	--	--	--	--	--	--	--	--	--	--	--	--	--	--	--	--	--	--	--	--	--	--	--	--	--	--	--	--	--	--	--	I	--	--	--	--	--	--	I	--	--	13
12						W	I	I	I	I	I	I	I	I	I	I	I	I	I	I	I	I	I	I	I	I	I	I	I	I	I	I	I	I	I	I	I	I	I	I	I	I	I	I	I	I	--	I	I	I	I	I	I	--	I	S	12
11					S	--	--	--	--	--	--	--	--	--	--	--	--	--	--	--	--	--	--	--	--	--	--	--	--	--	--	--	--	--	--	--	--	--	--	--	--	--	--	--	--	--	I	--	--	--	--	--	--	I	--	--	11
10					W	I	I	I	I	I	I	I	I	I	I	I	I	I	I	I	I	I	I	I	I	I	I	I	I	I	I	I	I	I	I	I	I	I	I	I	I	I	I	I	I	I	S										10
9				S	--	--	--	--	--	--	--	--	--	--	--	--	--	--	--	--	--	--	--	--	--	--	--	--	--	--	--	--	--	--	--	--	--	--	--	--	--	--	--	--	--	--	W										9
8				W	I	I	I	I	I	I	I	I	I	I	I	I	I	I	I	I	I	I	I	I	I	I	I	I	I	I	I	I	I	I	I	I	I	I	I	I	I	I	I	I	I	I	--	I	I	I	I	I	I	--	I	S	8
7			S	--	--	--	--	--	--	--	--	--	--	--	--	--	--	--	--	--	--	--	--	--	--	--	--	--	--	--	--	--	--	--	--	--	--	--	--	--	--	--	--	--	--	--	I	--	--	--	--	--	--	I	--	--	7
6			W	I	I	I	I	I	I	I	I	I	I	I	I	I	I	I	I	I	I	I	I	I	I	I	I	I	I	I	I	I	I	I	I	I	I	I	I	I	I	I	I	I	I	I	--	6	6	6	6	6	6	--	I	S	6
5		S	--	--	--	--	--	--	--	--	--	--	--	--	--	--	--	--	--	--	--	--	--	--	--	--	--	--	--	--	--	--	--	--	--	--	--	--	--	--	--	--	--	--	--	--	I	--	--	--	--	--	--	I	--	--	5
4		W	I	I	I	I	I	I	I	I	I	I	I	I	I	I	I	I	I	I	I	I	I	I	I	I	I	I	I	I	I	I	I	I	I	I	I	I	I	I	I	I	I	I	I	I	S										4
3	S	--	--	--	--	--	--	--	--	--	--	--	--	--	--	--	--	--	--	--	--	--	--	--	--	--	--	--	--	--	--	--	--	--	--	--	--	--	--	--	--	--	--	--	--	--	W										3
2	W	I	I	I	I	I	I	I	I	I	I	I	I	I	I	I	I	I	I	I	I	I	I	I	I	I	I	I	I	I	I	I	I	I	I	I	I	I	I	I	I	I	I	I	I	I	--	I	I	I	I	I	I	--	I	S	2
1	@	--	--	--	--	--	--	--	--	--	--	--	--	--	--	--	--	--	--	--	--	--	--	--	--	--	--	--	--	--	--	--	--	--	--	--	--	--	--	--	--	--	--	--	--	--	I	--	--	--	--	--	--	I	--	--	1
	56	55	54	53	52	51	50	49	48	47	46	45	44	43	42	41	40	39	38	37	36	35	34	33	32	31	30	29	28	27	26	25	24	23	22	21	20	19	18	17	16	15	14	13	12	11	10	9	8	7	6	5	4	3	2	1	

@ = Starting point   **I** = knit   **--** = purl   S = Slip   W = Wrap   **6** = 6 stitch cable

*The area shaded in **pink** is the section to omit when knitting the child size*

tippet scarf

This is a great project for beginners but also very satisfying and quick to knit up for more experienced knitters - especially when you are knitting with the yarn you have dyed yourself!

It is knitted in a "faux brioche". Brioche is a form of rib that involves slipped stitches and yarn overs. The faux (= fake!) brioche is made up of a clever combination of just knit and purl stitches, giving the overall impression of a real brioche.

The zig-zag texture is ideal for scarves and will hold its shape really well.

The addition of an opening in the shape of a vertical slit in the scarf is a nod back to the Victorian tippet - a small stole that has a loop at one end to allow weaving the other end through it to help keep it in place. By pulling one end of the scarf through the opening, it stays in place without the added bulk of a knot.

about this pattern

difficulty

measurements
12 cm (5 in) wide (unstretched),
length as desired

materials
Tall Yarns Superwash Merino DK
(225 m per 100 grams) or equivalent
double knitting yarn

metreage needed
1 hank knits a scarf of approx. 110 cm (43 in)

tension
30 sts and 30 rows measure 10 x 10 cm in
Faux Brioche

notions
one pair of 4.5 mm needles (since fit is not an issue for a scarf, it is not necessary to adjust needle size to achieve an exact gauge)

stitches

faux brioche:
Row 1: K3, P1
Row 2: K2, P1, K1

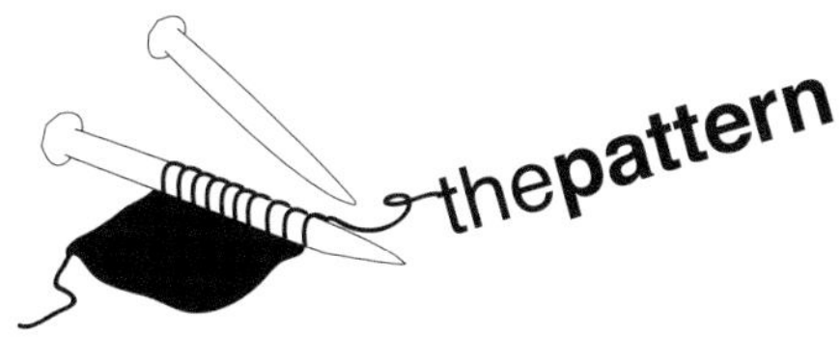

part 1

Cast on 35 sts
Row 1: S1, [K3, P1], repeat to the last 2 sts, K2
Row 2 onwards: as row 1

OPENING
When you have knitted to a height of approx. 30 cm (12 in), knit the opening as follows:

Row 1: S1, [K3, P1], repeat 3 times, K1 (18 sts), turn
Row 2: S1, K2, P1, [K3, P1], repeat twice, K2
Note: you are only knitting across half of all stitches. The remaining stitches just remain on the needle.
Repeat these 2 rows to a height of approx. 8 cm (3 in)
Now cut the yarn you are knitting with, leaving an end of approx. 10 cm (4 in).
Leave the 18 sts you have been knitting on your needle.
Now you will knit the second part of the opening.

You start knitting at the middle of the work (at the base of the opening). Leave an end of approx. 10 cm (4 in) of yarn to weave in later.

Row 1: S1, M1, K1, P1, [K3, P1], repeat twice, K2 (18 sts), turn
Row 2: S1, [K3, P1], repeat 3 times, K1
Row 3: S1, K2, P1, [K3, P1], repeat twice, K2

Repeat these 2 rows until you have reached the same height as the other half of the opening, finishing with an even row. Continue knitting this row by knitting the 18 sts that have been waiting, as follows:

K2tog, K2, P1, [K3, p1], repeat twice, K2 (35 sts)

part 2

Proceed by knitting the rows as you did in part 1.

Continue in the Faux Brioche until you are near to finishing your ball of yarn or to the desired length. Cast off all sts loosely.

Weave in all ends, ensuring you tie off the loose ends at either end of the opening firmly before weaving them in.

dyeing recipe

Follow the dyeing instructions for dyeing stripes, chapter 6. When winding the long hank, place the seats of the chairs you are winding the yarn around approx. 88 cm / 34.5 in apart on the table. When you dye half the hank at this length, you will achieve a similar stripy effect to the scarf in the picture. The colours used for this scarf were Sage and Pale Pumpkin. They were combined in a dish (and squidged together a lot) to create this blended, soft colour.

baby blanket

This blanket is knitted in a combination of stocking, moss and garter stitches so that it is completely double sided. It was inspired by one of Helen's quilts, made with home-dyed cotton in the same graduated colour palette. What better way to show off graduated colours as dyed in Chapter 4. Although the blanket looks as though it was made up out of a huge number of small squares, it is actually knitted in long strips that can either be knitted together with every subsequent strip or sewn together at the end of the project.

about this pattern

difficulty

sizes
Approx. 90 x 100 cm (36 x 40 in)

materials
650 grams Tall Yarns Superwash Merino DK (225 m per 100 grams) or equivalent double-knitting yarn

metreage needed
Approx. 1450 m

tension
20 sts and 28 rows measure 10 x 10 cm (4 x 4 in) in stocking stitch

notions
one pair of 4.0 mm needles (or bigger or smaller to help you achieve gauge)
one 4.0 mm circular needle of 120 cm (47 in)

stitches

moss stitch: K1, P1 (alternating in subsequent rows)
stocking stitch: One row K, one row P
garter stitch: All rows K

the pattern

Using the finished project picture as your colour chart, start in the top left corner of the picture and work from left to right (the blanket is shown lying sideways).
Cast on 17 sts with colour 1 (the dark tie and dye yarn).

block 1

Row 1 – 3: moss st (K1, P1, ending with a K st).
Row 4: 3 sts moss (K1, P1, K1), K11, 3 sts moss (K1, P1, K1).
Row 5: 3 sts moss (K1, P1, K1), P11, 3 sts moss (K1, P1, K1).
Repeat rows 4 and 5 a total of 6 times.
Row 18: as row 4.
Row 19 – 21: moss st (as rows 1 – 3).
Change to the next colour (the darkest solid-coloured yarn).
Row 22: K.

block 2

Rows 23 – 25: as rows 19 – 21.
Row 26: 3 sts moss (K1, P1, K1), P11, 3 sts moss (K1, P1, K1).
Row 27: 3 sts moss (K1, P1, K1), K11, 3 sts moss (K1, P1, K1).
Repeat rows 26 and 27 a total of 6 times.
Row 40: as row 26.
Rows 41 – 43: moss st.
Row 44: K.
Change to the next colour, knit 1 row and repeat Block 1.
Change colour, K 1 row, repeat Block 2.
Repeat these 2 blocks until you have knitted all the squares in the first row.
Cast off all sts.

Start the next row, making sure you start with Block 2, so that the direction of the st.st panels alternates throughout the blanket.
Continue knitting the strips until you have finished them all.

NOTE: there are 2 options for making up the blanket.
Option 1: When you knit strip 2, pick up 1 st from the edge of strip 1 at the start of each even row and knit it together with the first stitch of that row. When you finish strip 2, strip 1 will be attached along the entire side.
Option 2: knit all strips separately, then sew them together when you have finished the last strip.

finishing

With the circular needle, pick up 221 sts along one side of the blanket.
Knit 4 rows in garter st, as follows:
K1, M1, K to 1 st from end of row, M1, K1.
Knit all 4 rows like this.
Repeat this for all 4 sides of the blanket.
Sew up the corners.
Lightly block the blanket with a warm, steamy iron.

dyeing recipe

Divide the yarn into 6 hanks of 100 grams and 1 hank of 50 grams.
Prepare 2 of the 100 grams hanks as for tie-and-dye (chapter 8).
All hanks will be dyed using the graduated dyeing technique described in Chapter 4. Make 500 ml of dye solution. Follow the dyeing instructions on page 28, putting in one of the tie and dye hanks first and the other tie and dye hank last. Dye the extra 50 grams hank separately in a strong solution of the same colour.

chunky beret

I had such fun designing this beret. It's fast and easy and very striking.

Because the chunky yarn has lots of give, it is not as easy to determine the exact number of stitches you need for a perfect fit. That's where the ribbon comes in. Not only does it add to the flair of the hat, it also guarantees a perfect fit. You can either buy a coloured ribbon or use a white or cream coloured silk ribbon and add it to the yarn when you soak it. Then dye it together with the yarn for a colour-coordinated finish. If you really do not like a ribbon, then thread through a piece of the yarn you've used to knit the hat and tie that off at the right size for your head. If you keep the ends on the inside of the hat, you won't be able to see the tie and you'll still be able to adjust it in the future if you want to.

The pattern works well with space-dyed or solid-coloured yarns, but can be knitted in a stripy yarn as well. Do keep in mind that the more varied the colours of the yarn, the less you'll notice the moss stitch panels.

about this pattern

difficulty

●●●

measurements
When lying flat, the beret measures 30 cm (12 in) across. The head circumference is variable depending on how you tie off the ribbon.

materials
Tall Yarns BFL chunky (100 m per 100 grams) or equivalent chunky yarn

metreage needed
Approx. 160 m

tension
12 sts and 19 rows measure 10 x 10 cm. in st.st

notions
one set of 8 mm DPN's (20 cm / 8 in long)

stitches

picot cast on: [Cast on 5 sts using the cable cast-on method, cast off 2 sts, slip st on RH needle back onto LH needle] (3 sts now on LH needle), repeat until desired number of sts has been achieved (generally a multiple of 3).
stocking stitch: One row K, one row P
moss stitch: K1, P1 (alternating in subsequent rows)

thepattern

Cast on 54 sts using the picot cast-on method (15 sts on needles 1 and 2, 12 sts on needles 3 and 4). Redistribute the sts to 14 sts on needles 1 and 3 and 13 on needles 2 and 4. Join the sts in the round.

Round 1 – 6: *P1, K2, repeat to end of round
Round 7: *P1, K1, M1, K1, repeat to end of round (72sts)
Redistribute sts so that every needle has 18 sts
Round 8: *K5, M1, K9, M1, K4, repeat 3 times to end of round (80sts)
Round 9: *K5, M1, P1, M1, K9, M1, P1, M1, K4* x 4 (96sts)
Round 10: *K5, M1, P1, K1, P1, M1, K9, M1, P1, K1, P1, M1, K4* x 4 (112sts)
Round 11: *K5, M1, [P1, K1] x 2, P1, M1, K9, M1, [P1, K1] x 2, P1, M1, K4* x 4 (128sts)
Round 12: *K5, [P1, K1] x 3, P1, K9, [P1, K1] x 3, P1, K4* x 4
Round 13: *K5, [K1, P1] x 3, K10, [K1, P1] x 3, K5* x 4
Round 14: as round 12
Round 15: *K5, M1, [K1, P1] x 3, K1, M1, K9, M1, [K1, P1] x 3, K1, M1, K4* x 4 (144sts)
Round 16: *K5, [K1, P1] x 4, K10, [K1, P1] x 4, K5* x 4
Round 17: *K5, [P1, K1] x 4, P1, K9, [P1, K1] x 4, P1, K4* x 4
Round 18 – 21: repeat rows 16/17 twice
Round 22: *K5, P2tog, [K1, P1] x 2, K1, P2tog, K9, P2tog, [K1, P1] x 2, K1, P2tog, K4 * x 4 (128sts)
Round 23: *K5, [K1, P1] x 3, K10, [K1, P1] x 3, K5* x 4
Round 24: *K5, [P1, K1] x 3, P1, K9, [P1, K1] x 3, P1, K4* x 4
Round 25: as row 23
Round 26: *K5, K2tog, P1, K1, P1, S1, K1, PSSO, K9, K2tog, P1, K1, P1, S1, K1, PSSO, K4* x 4
Round 27: *K5, [P1, K1] x 2, P1, K9, [P1, K1] x 2, P1, K4* x 4
Round 28: *K5, [K1, P1] x 2, K10, [K1, P1] x 2, K5* x 4
Round 29: as round 27
Round 30: *K5, P2tog, K1, P2tog, K9, P2tog, K1, P2tog, K4* x 4
Round 31: *K6, P1, K11, P1, K5* x 4
Round 32: *K5, P1, K1, P1, K9, P1, K1, P1, K4* x 4
Round 33: as round 31
Round 34: *K5, S1, K2tog, PSSO, K9, S1, K2tog, PSSO, K4* x 4
Round 35: *K5, P1, K9, P1, K4* x 4
Round 36: K
Round 37: as round 35
Round 38: *K4, S1, K2tog, PSSO, K7, S1, K2tog, PSSO, K3* x 4
Round 39: *K4, P1, K7, P1, K3* x 4
Round 40: K
Round 41: as round 39
Round 42: *K3, S1, K2tog, PSSO, K5, S1, K2tog, PSSO, K2* x 4
Round 43: *K3, P1, K5, P1, K2* x 4
Round 44: K
Round 45: as round 43
Round 46: *K2, S1, K2tog, PSSO, K3, S1, K2tog, PSSO, K1* x 4
Round 47: *K2, P1, K3, P1, K1* x 4
Round 48: K
Round 49: as round 47
Round 50: *K1, S1, K2tog, PSSO, K1, S1, K2tog, PSSO* x 4
Round 47: [K1, P1] x 8
Round 48: K
Round 49: as round 47
Round 50: *S1, K2tog, PSSO, P1* x 4 (8 sts)
Round 51: *S1, K2tog, PSSO, P1* x 2 (4 sts)
Cast off the last 4 sts and cut off the yarn leaving approx. 15 cm (6 in) of yarn.

finishing

Centre: use the end of yarn to weave through and pull together the centre 4 sts. Weave in end.
Rim: use the end of yarn to tidy up the point where you started knitting in the round and weave in the end of yarn. Weave the ribbon (or some yarn) through the rim of the beret (at the point where you started increasing stitches works best) and tie off the yarn or tie the ribbon in a nice bow.

dyeing recipe

The red beret was dyed in a dish (chapter 2) in the microwave using Plum and Winter Red, with a medium amount of squidging to mix up the colours (i.e. don't keep them separate but don't mix them up completely either). The blue beret was also dyed in the microwave using only Slate.

kids' tanktop

This pattern is suitable for less experienced knitters. The only stitches used are knit and purl and there is some decreasing involved, but that's just about it. Extra interest can be added by using a different colour of yarn for the edges along the bottom, armholes and neck, which are all knitted in a single rib (1 stitch knit, 1 stitch purl).

What makes this top interesting is what happens when you knit it with your own dyed yarn, especially when you've used a special dyeing technique like the ones in chapters 6, 7 or 8. For example, you can dye a striped yarn using no more than 2 colours. But by overlapping the colours in the middle of the hank, you create a third colour that separates the 2 main colours of the stripes, creating an interesting effect. If you'd rather stick to 2 colours only, the dyeing process is the same. You just don't overlap them when dyeing.

about this pattern

difficulty

sizes
3 – 5 yrs (116 cm / 46 in total height)
7 – 8 yrs (approx. 128 cm / 50 in)
9 – 10 yrs (approx. 140 cm / 55 in).

garment
Back length from base of neck approx.
measurements: 40 (45, 50) cm / 15.5 (17.5, 19.5) in

chest circumference
65 (70, 75) cm / 25.5 (27.5, 29.5) in.

materials
150 - 200 grams Tall Yarns Superwash Merino DK (225 m per 100 grams) or equivalent double knitting yarn

metreage needed
Approx. 350 - 400 m

tension
20 sts and 28 rows measure 10 x 10 cm (4 x 4 in) in stocking stitch

notions
one pair of 4.0 mm needles (or bigger or smaller to help you achieve gauge)

stitches

single rib: K1, P1.
stocking stitch: One row K, one row P.

the pattern

back

Cast on 61 (76, 81) sts.
Rows 1 – 10: Knit in single rib.
Row 11: S1, M1, K to the last st, M1, K1 (63, 78, 83 sts).
Row 12: S1, P to end of row.
Knit in St. St. to a total height of 23 (27, 30) cm.

ARM OPENING
(RS) Row 1: cast off (bind off) the first 6 (7, 7) sts knitwise, K rest of row (57, 71, 76 sts).
(WS) Row 2: bind off the first 6 (7, 7) sts purlwise, P rest of row (51, 64, 69 sts).
Row 3: K first st tog, K to last 2 sts, SSK (49, 62, 67 sts).
Repeat this row 5 (6, 6) times.
At the end of Row 8 (9, 9) you should have 39 (50, 55) sts left on your needle.
K to a total height of 39 (44, 49) cm, ending with a P row.
Next row: S1, K6 (7, 8), bind off 25 (34, 37) sts, K 7 (8, 9).
Work 2 more rows with the remaining 7 (8, 9) sts of what will be the left shoulder (leaving the 7 (8, 9) sts on the other side of the neck opening on the needle).
Last row: (RS) K and bind off all 7 (8, 9) sts.
Now rejoin the yarn to knit the other 7 (8, 9) shoulder sts.

Note: if you are knitting with a stripey yarn, wind off the ball to find the repeat of the colouring at the same point it was when you knitted the last st before binding off the neck stitches, so both shoulder pieces end up looking the same, as in the picture.

Work 2 more rows with the remaining 7 (8, 9) sts of what will become the right shoulder.
Last row: (RS) K and bind off all 7 (8, 9) sts.

front

Knit as back until the start of the arm openings.

ARM OPENING
(RS) Row 1: bind off the first 6 (7, 7) sts knitwise, K rest of row (57, 71, 76 sts).
(WS) Row 2: bind off the first 5 (7, 6) sts purlwise, P rest of row (52, 64, 70 sts).
Row 3: K first st tog, K to last 2 sts, SSK (50, 62, 68 sts).
Repeat this row 5 (6, 6) times.
At the end of Row 8 (9, 9) you should have 40 (50, 56) sts left on your needle.
Next row (RS): S1, K17 (22, 25), SSK, K2tog, K18 (23, 26). Total 38 (48, 54) sts.
The last 24 sts you have knitted will go on to form the front right shoulder part.
Next row: S1, P18 (23, 26)
Now place the other 24 sts (which will go on to become the front left shoulder part) onto a spare needle, a stitch holder or a piece of scrap yarn in a contrasting colour, so they can be kept out of the way while you go on knitting the front right shoulder.
Next K row: K2tog, K to end of row.
Next P row: S1, P to end of row.
Repeat these 2 rows until you have 7 (8, 9) sts left
Now K to the correct total height, i.e. ensuring that the number of rows of the armhole matches the number of rows of the armhole of the back panel, finishing with a WS row.

In the next row, bind off all sts.
Now pick up the sts of the left front shoulder panel. Again, if you are knitting with a self-striping yarn, ensure you unwind the ball until you match the repeat with where you had left off just before you knitted the first 2 sts together in the middle.
Rejoin the yarn, starting on the WS with a P row, S1, P to end of row.
Next row: S1, K to the last 2 sts, SSK.
Next row: S1, P to end of row.
Repeat these 2 rows until you have 7 (8, 9) sts left on the needle.
Now K to the correct total height, i.e. ensuring that the number of rows of the armhole matches the number of rows of the armhole of the back panel, finishing with a WS row. In the next row, bind off all sts.

arm edgings

Join shoulder seams, using a mattress stitch (see page 95).
Pick up (94, 100, 110) sts along the edge of the armhole, starting with the left arm. Your starting point is the point on the back where you started decreasing sts for the armhole. Check that you have approx. half the number of sts you need to pick up when you pass the shoulder seam. Continue along the front panel until you get to the point where you started decreasing for the armhole when knitting the front.
*K 1 row.
In the next row, start a single rib (K1, P1).
K 7 (8, 9) more rows in single rib, binding off all sts as they present themselves in the last row*
For the right armhole, start picking up sts on the front panel, ending up at the base of the armhole on the back.
Repeat instructions from * to *.

neck edge

Pick up (32, 40, 44) sts along the back neck edge and place them on a double pointed needle (DPN – needle 1). K all 32 (40, 44) sts.
Now pick up 34 (36, 40) sts along the left front neck edge, place on a double pointed needle (needle 2) and K them.
Repeat on the right front neck edge (needle 3).
You now have a total of 100 (112, 124) sts, divided over 3 needles.
In the following round, start a K1, P1 rib.
Work the back neck edge sts, then the front left neck edge until you have 2 more sts on needle 2, K2tog.
Now start needle 3 as follows:
SSK, continue the round, starting with a P st after your SSK.
Round 2, 4, 6: knit or purl each stitch as it presents itself, making sure that you Knit the 2 sts that make up the middle front of the V-neck (if you purl them, it will not look as tidy).
Round 3, 5, 7: K1, P1 along needle 1, K1, P1 along needle 2 until you have 2 sts left on needle 2, K2tog, start needle 3 with SSK, then P1, K1 until you've finished the round.
Round 8: as round 7, casting off all sts after knitting or purling them.

finishing

Close both side seams using mattress stitch; work in all ends.

dyeing recipe

Follow the dyeing instructions for dyeing stripes, chapter 6. To establish the length of your hank, cast on the right number of sts for the size of the garment you will be knitting and knit 4 rows. Frog back (= rip back, pull out) 3 rows, remembering to place markers. Measure the distance between your markers. This distance = half the total length of your hank. When dyeing, overlap the 2 colours in the middle by dyeing close to 2/3 of the hank with Turmeric, then dying 2/3 of the hank with Autumn Sky (the area of overlap in the middle will be green at the end of the second dye-cycle). (See version one on page 41).

boucle bodywarmer

This pattern demands some more knitting experience, especially when using bouclé knitting yarn. The whole idea with bouclé is that you can't make out the stitches. This means that while knitting, you really need to keep exact track of where you've got to (e.g. by writing down your progress), or you won't remember where you were and, unlike with a regular WIP (work in progress), you can't quickly look back over your work to find your place in the pattern. The gradual decreases and increases along the edges of the front and back panels make for a lovely fitted look but demand you to be scrupulous in your progress tracking! This project is the perfect way to show off tie and dye knitting with clips as explained in chapter 8, as the bobbles show the bright sections as little jewels on a multi-coloured dark base. The wide variety of colours means that you can throw on this extra layer over just about anything, which is exactly what its intended use is!

about this pattern

difficulty

sizes
Women's size UK 6 – 8 (S; US 2 - 4), 10 – 14 (M; US 6 - 10), 16 – 20 (L; US 12 - 16)

garment
Back length approx. 67 cm / 26.5 in (S), 70 cm / 27.5 in (M, L)

measurements
Chest: 98 cm / 38.5 in (S), 108 cm / 43.5 in (M), 118 cm / 46.5 in (L)
Waist: 80 cm / 31.5 in (S), 90 cm / 35.5 in (M), 100 cm / 39.5 in (L)
Hips: 100 cm / 39.5 in (S), 110 cm / 43 in (M), 120 cm / 47 in (L)

materials
400 - 500 grams Tall Yarns Superwash Merino Bouclé (100 m per 100 grams) or equivalent bouclé yarn

metreage needed
Approx. 400 - 500m

tension
11 sts and 16 rows measure 10 x 10 cm in Twisted Stocking Stitch

notions
one pair of 5.5 mm needles (or bigger or smaller to help you achieve gauge)

stitches

twisted stocking stitch (t.st.st): All K rows, K every stitch through its back loop (instead of its front loop, as you would do with a normal st.st.). All P rows, regular P sts.

the pattern

Note: in this pattern, the purl side of the work is the right side (RS) unlike most projects knitted in st.st. The purl side gives the nicest bobbled effect and the least stitch definition.

back

Cast on 55 (61, 65) sts.
Work 15 (17, 17) cm in twisted st.st, ending with a RS row.
Next row: S1, K2tog, K twisted sts to 3 sts from the end of the row, SSK, K1T (Knit 1 st Twisted).
Next 5 rows: S1, work to end of row.
Repeat these 6 rows 3 times (47, 53, 57 sts).
Next row: S1, K2tog, K t.st.st. to 3 sts from end, SSK, K1T (45, 51, 55 sts).
Work 7 (9, 9) rows in t.st.st.
Next row: S1, M1, K t.st.st. to last st, M1, K1T.
Next 5 rows: S1, work to end of row.
Repeat these 6 rows twice (51, 57, 61 sts).
Next row: S1, M1, K t.st.st. to last st, M1, K1T (53, 59, 63 sts).
K 3 rows in t.st.st.

ARM OPENING
Next 2 rows: cast off 3 (4,5) sts at the start of the row (47, 51, 53 sts).
Next 2 rows: dec. 1 st. at each end of the row (43, 47, 49 sts).
Next row: S1, K t.st.st. to end.
Next row: dec. 1 st. at each end of the row (41, 45, 47 sts).
Work until the total arm opening measures 20 cm in height, ending with a RS row.
Next 4 rows: cast off first 5 (6, 6) sts, work to end of row (21, 21, 23 sts).
Next row: cast off remaining 21 (21, 23) sts.

right front

Cast on 29 (32, 34) sts.
Work 15 (17, 17) cm in twisted st. st, ending with a RS row.
Next row: S1, K2tog, work to end of row.
Next 5 rows: S1, work to end of row.
Repeat these 6 rows 3 times (25, 28, 30 sts).
Next row: S1, K2tog, work to end of row (24, 27, 29 sts).
Work 7 (9, 9) rows in t.st.st.
Next row: S1, M1, work to end of row.
Next 5 rows: S1, work to end of row.
Repeat these 6 rows twice (27, 30, 32 sts).
Next row: S1, M1, work to end of row (28, 31, 33 sts).
K 3 rows in t.st.st.

ARM OPENING AND NECK LINE
Row 1 (WS): cast off 3 (4, 5) sts, work to end of row (25, 27, 28 sts).
Row 2 (RS): cast off 4 sts, work to end of row (21, 23, 24 sts).
Row 3 (WS): cast off 2 sts, work to end of row (19, 21, 22 sts).
Row 4 (RS): S1, work to end of row.
Row 5 (WS): S1, work to 3 sts from end, K2tog, K1T (18, 20, 21 sts).
Repeat the last 2 rows until you have 10 (12, 13) sts left.
Work on until the total height of the armhole is 1 cm shorter than the arm opening of the back, ending with a WS row.
Next row: cast off 5 (6, 7) sts, work to end.
Next row: P.
Next row: cast off all remaining sts.

left front

Knit as a mirror image of the right front panel.

collar

First sew up both shoulders using mattress stitch. If you find it difficult to use the original bouclé yarn, then use a smoother yarn in a colour that blends in with your bouclé.
Pick up 28 sts along the neckline of the right front panel (starting at the mid front), then 26 sts along the back neck and another 28 sts along the left front.
Row 1: P to 3 sts from end, ytb, S1, turn.
Row 2: wrap the slipped st by moving ytb again, S1, K t.st.st to 3 sts from end, ytf, S1, turn.
Row 3: wrap the slipped st by moving ytf again, P to 6 sts from end of row, ytb, S1, turn.
Row 4: wrap the slipped st by moving ytb again, S1, K t.st.st to 6 sts from end, ytf, S1, turn.
Row 5: wrap the slipped st by moving ytf again, P to 9 sts from end of row, ytb, S1, turn.
Row 6: wrap the slipped st by moving ytb again, S1, K t.st.st to 9 sts from end, ytf, S1, turn.
Row 7: wrap the slipped st by moving ytf again, P to 12 sts from end of row, ytb, S1, turn.
Row 8: wrap the slipped st by moving ytb again, S1, K t.st.st to 12 sts from end, ytf, S1, turn.
Row 9: P to end of row.
Row 10: K t.st.st to end of row.
Row 11: P to end of row.
Row 12: Cast off all sts loosely.

finishing

Close both side seams using mattress stitch (see page 94); work in all ends.
Fold over the front edges of the collar (on either side of the mid front line) and sew them down with a couple of sts. Leave the rest of the collar to roll over by itself.

optional

Add a closure by

- sewing a couple of silk or satin ribbons on either side at waist level or
- knit an I-cord in the same bouclé yarn (see page 95)
  or
- add hooks and eyes if you want your closure to be invisible

dyeing recipe

The project in the picture was dyed using acid dyes in the colours turquoise, lemon yellow and cerise in "The Tweed Effect", p. 54.

simple socks

A basic sock pattern to show off your own dyed yarn.

about this pattern

difficulty
If you've knitted socks before: easy

If these are your first socks: intermediate

measurements
The number of stitches used is suitable to knit socks of sizes 3-4 and up

materials
100 grams of sock yarn

metreage needed
Approx. 400 metres

tension
32 sts and 50 rows measure 10 x 10 cm in stocking stitch

notions
One pair of 2.5 mm needles (if necessary, use bigger or smaller to achieve the right gauge)
Optional: 1 stitch holder and 2 stitch markers

stitches

stocking stitch:
(st.st.) K on RS, P on WS
rib: K2, P2

the pattern

cuff

Cast on 60 sts divided over 4 needles (15 sts. per needle)
Rounds 1-20: Rib

leg

Round 21 onwards: K
Knit to a total height of approx. 20 cm (8 in) or to your own preferred height – the point where you start the heel is just about where your ankle sticks out on the outside of your leg.

heel

The heel is knitted with half of all sts (30), so only the sts on needles 1 and 2.
Leave the other sts on needles 3 and 4 OR transfer them to a stitch holder OR onto a spare piece of yarn in a contrasting colour
Row 1: S1, K29, turn
Row 2: S1, P29, turn
Continue in st.st. on these 30 sts for 28 more rows
Row 31: S1, K16, SKPO, K1, turn
Row 32: S1, P5, P2tog, P1, turn
Row 33: S1, K to 1 st before the gap, SKPO, K1, turn
Row 34: S1, P to 1 st before the gap, P2tog, P1, turn
Repeat the last 2 rows until all the sts have been worked (16 sts)
Next round: K the 16 sts, then pick up and knit 15 sts from the heel flap, [place a stitch marker if you find it useful], knit the stitches on needles 3 and 4 (transfer them onto the needles first if they've been on a stitch holder or a spare piece of yarn), [place another stitch marker], pick up and knit 15 sts up the other side of the heel flap, then knit 8 more sts (i.e. halfway through the 16 sts that form the bottom of the heel)
Note: needles 1 and 2 have 23 heel stitches each on them and needles 3 and 4 have 15 stitches each on them
Next round: K to 3 sts before the first stitch marker, K2tog, K1, K across needles 3 and 4 (to the 2nd stitch marker), K1, SKPO, K to end of round
Next round: K
Repeat these last 2 rounds until you have 15 sts left on each needle (= 60 sts across all needles)

foot

Continue knitting round until you reach the desired length, which is the measurement of the foot from the heel to the tip of the big toe, minus 5 cm (2 in).

toe

Next round, starting at the beginning of needle 1: [K1, SKPO, K to 3 sts before the end of needle 2, K2tog, K1], repeat this across needles 3 and 4
Do check that you are decreasing your stitches in the correct places, i.e. to the sides of your toes, not on top and underneath!
Next round: K
Repeat these 2 rounds until you have 24 sts remaining (6 per needle)
Cast-off either using the Kitchener Stitch, or the 3-needle cast off method (see p. 94).
Weave in all loose ends or cast on the next sock first to avoid "second sock syndrome"!
(see p.86)

dyeing recipe

The following colours and techniques were used for the socks in the picture (working from the front to the back):
Rust sock: painted (chapter 7) in Turmeric and Paprika
Rust/mustard sock: painted (chapter 7) in Turmeric and Paprika
Purple/blue sock: painted (chapter 7) in Plum and Slate
Purple sock: dyed in a dish (chapter 2) in Plum and Autumn Sky

three seasons cardigan

Relaxed cardigan that can be knitted in a wide variety of yarns and textures. Because of the simple shape of the cardigan, it fits from a size 8 all the way up to a 16 without having to amend the pattern. Since it has a one-button closure, it would lend itself really well to a space-dyed yarn that is dyed to match the colours of a special, unique button. The pattern is for an Aran yarn, knitted on 4.5 mm needles. The sleeves of the cardigan are knitted simultaneously and top-down to allow using up all the yarn you have available; if you have more, you can opt to knit longer sleeves, if you have a little less, the sleeves are left a bit shorter. Because you use up your yarn on the sleeves, you knit the edging for the neckline before knitting the sleeves.

about this pattern

difficulty

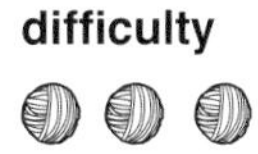

measurements
chest 100 cm (40 in)
back length: 52 cm (20.5 in)

materials
Tall Yarns Alpaca Silk (166 m. per 100 grams) or equivalent Aran yarn

metreage needed
Approx. 830 m. (500 grams)

tension
19 sts and 25 rows measure 10 x 10 cm

notions
one pair of 4.5 mm needles

stitches

single rib: K1, P1
stocking stitch: One row K, one row P

thepattern

back

Loosely cast on 100 sts
K 7 rows in st.st. (ending with a K row)
Row 8: K
Rows 9 onward: st.st. to a total height of 35 cm

Note: there are 2 options for creating the hemlines of the back and front panels. Option 1: you can knit the hem together with your stitches in row 15 by knitting each subsequent cast-on loop together with the corresponding stitch. If these instructions baffle you, go for Option 2: knit to the requested height of 35 cm and follow the hemline instructions under "finishing".

ARMHOLES
Row 1: at each end of row, cast off 5 sts (90 sts)
Row 2 and all other even rows: P
Rows 3, 5, 7: S2, K1, PSSO, K to 3 sts from end of row, K2tog, K1 (84 sts)
Row 9: K
Row 11: as 3, 5, 7 (82 sts)
Row 13: K
Row 15: as row 11 (80 sts)
K to a total height of 54 cm, ending with a WS row

NECKLINE AND SHOULDERS
Next row (RS): S1, K27, cast off 24 sts, K to end of row
You now have 2 sets of 28 sts on your needle.
Working with the first set of 28 sts, finish the left shoulder as follows:
Rows 1, 3, 5, 7 (WS): S1, P to end of row
Row 2 (RS): cast off 4 sts, K to end of row (24 sts)
Rows 4, 6: cast off 3 sts, K to end of row (8 sts)
Row 8: cast off 1 st, K to end of row (17 sts)
Row 9: cast off 10 sts, P to end (7 sts)
Row 10: K
Row 11: cast off last 7 sts.
Now turn your attention to the second set of 28 sts, which still remain on your needle.
Row 1 (WS): cast off 4 sts, P to end (24 sts)
Rows 2, 4, 6: S1, K to end
Rows 3, 5: cast off 3 sts, P to end (18 sts)
Row 7: cast off 1 sts, P to end (17 sts)
Row 8: cast off 10 sts, K to end (7 sts)
Row 9: S1, P to end
Row 10: cast off 7 remaining sts

right front panel

Loosely cast on 51 sts
K 7 rows in st.st. (ending with a K row)
Row 8: K
Rows 9 - 15: st.st. (note for experienced knitters: creating the hem by picking up the cast-on sts as per the back, see above, in the last row)
Row 16: S1, P to end of row, add 4 sts by casting on 4 sts using the cable cast-on method (55 sts)
Rows 17 onward: st.st to a total height of 35 cm

RIGHT ARMHOLE
Row 1 and all following uneven rows: S1, K to end of row
Row 2: cast off 5 sts, P to end of row (50 sts)
Row 4, 6, 8: S1, P2tog, P to end of Row (47 sts)
Row 10: S1, P to end of row
Row 12: as rows 4, 6, 8 (46 sts)
Row 14: S1, P to end of row
Row 16: as row 12 (45 sts)
Work next 6 rows in st.st

NECKLINE AND SHOULDERS
Row 1: cast off first 3 sts, K to end of row
Row 2: S1, P27, W&T
Row 3 and all uneven rows to follow: SWS, K to end of row
Row 4: S1, P24, W&T
Row 6: S1, P23, W&T
Row 8: S1, P22, W&T
Row 10: S1, P21, W&T
Row 12: S1, P20, W&T
Row 14: S1, P19, W&T
Row 16: S1, P18, W&T
Row 18: S1, P17, W&T
Row 20: S1, P17, W&T
Row 22 onwards: st.st to a total height of 57 cm, ending with a RS row
Next row (WS): cast off 10 sts, P to end
Next row: S1, K to end
Next row: cast off 7 remaining sts
Place the remaining sts along the neckline on a spare needle, needle holder or scrap piece of yarn.

left front panel

Loosely cast on 51 sts
K 7 rows in st.st (ending with a K row)
Row 8: K
Rows 9 - 16: st.st (as per the back, you have the option of creating the hem by picking up the cast-on stitches or hemming afterwards)
Row 17: S1, K to end of row, add 4 sts by casting on 4 sts using the cable cast-on method (55 sts)
Rows 18 onward: st.st. to a total height of 35 cm

left armhole

Row 1: cast off 5 sts, K to end of row (50 sts)
Row 2 and all uneven rows: S1, P to end of row
Row 3, 5, 7: S2, K1, PSSO, K to end of Row (47 sts)
Row 9: S1, K to end of row
Row 11: as rows 3,5,7 (46 sts)
Row 13: S1, K to end of row
Row 15: as row 11 (45 sts)
Work next 7 rows in st.st, casting off the first 3 sts of the last row (42 sts)

NECKLINE AND SHOULDERS
Row 1: S1, K27, W&T
Rows 2 and all even rows to follow: SWS, P to end of row
Row 3: S1, K24, W&T
Row 5: S1, K23, W&T
Row 7: S1, K22, W&T
Row 9: S1, K21, W&T
Row 11: S1, K20, W&T
Row 13: S1, K19, W&T
Row 15: S1, K18, W&T
Row 17: S1, K17, W&T
Row 19: S1, K17, W&T
Row 21 onwards: st.st to a total height of 57 cm, ending with a WS row
Next row (RS): cast off 10 sts, K to end
Next row: S1, P to end
Next row: cast off 7 remaining sts
Place the remaining sts along the neckline on a spare needle, needle holder or scrap piece of yarn.

NECKLINE
Sew shoulder seams.
With a 4.5 mm needle (or thinner if you find that easier), pick up 52 sts along the neckline of the left front panel, 61 sts along the back neckline and another 52 sts along the neckline of the right front panel (165 sts)
Row 1: S1, K4, *P1, K1, repeat from * to last 6 sts, P1, K5
Rows 2-6: S1, work all sts as they present themselves
Row 7: S1, K4, *P1, K1, P1, S1, K2tog, PSSO, repeat from * 24 times, P1, K1, P1, K1, P1, K5 (115 sts)
Row 8: S1, P4, [K1, P1] to 6 sts before the end of the row, K1, P5
Row 9: knit all sts as they present themselves
Row 10: knit all sts as they present themselves until 10 sts remain, cast off the next 3** sts, P1, K1, P5
Row 11: S1, K4, P1, K1, cast on 3** sts, P1, K1, etc.
Knit 7 more rows, all sts as they present themselves
Cast off all sts loosely in the next row.

** casting off 3 sts allows for a button as big as 4 cm (1.5 in) across. For a smaller button, cast off fewer sts. If unsure, knit a small sample in a K1, P1 rib and knit a 2 st buttonhole into it. If that is still too big, consider increasing the size of your button or making 2 buttonholes, one in row 7 and one in row 13.

TIP

to ensure a loose cast off, you can knit the last row on a much bigger needle (e.g. 7 mm). This ensures your last row of sts are bigger, giving a looser cast-off edge.

sleeves

Cast on 11 sts
Row 1: S1, K10, cast on 5 sts (using cable cast-on method) (16 sts)
Row 2: S1, P15, cast on 5 (21 sts)
Row 3: S1, M1, K to last st, M1, K1 (23 sts)
Row 4: S1, M1, P to last st, M1, P1 (25 sts)
Repeat the last 2 rows until you have 31 sts on the needles
Row 8: S1, P to end of row
Row 9: S1, M1, K to last st, M1, K1 (33 sts)
Repeat these 2 rows until you have 55 sts on your needle, ending with a RS row
Row 32: S1, M1, P to last st, M1, P1 (57 sts)
Row 33: S1, M1, K to last st, M1, K1 (59 sts)
Repeat these last rows 3 times (71 sts)
Row 40: S1, P to end of row, cast on 4 sts (75 sts)
Row 41: S1, K to end of row, cast on 4 sts (79 sts)

Note: this pattern specifies 500 grams of yarn. If you are working with 5 balls of 100 grams or 5 hanks of 100 grams, there will come a time when you are working your last ball of yarn. Once at that point, knit one sleeve from the centre of the ball and one from the outside or rewind the ball into 2 smaller (equal-sized) balls.

Now cast on the second sleeve.
Work the first 41 rows as above.
Proceed with both sleeves in st.st, ensuring you knit the same number of rows for both sleeves, ending with a RS row once you have approx. 15 grams of yarn left.
Next row (WS): K
Next row (RS): K
Proceed with a further 5 rows of st.st
Next row: cast off all sts loosely

finishing

Carefully block the panels and sleeves. If you are not familiar with blocking, iron them on the back with your iron on a cool setting, with steam if possible. Do not press down hard on your knitting as this will affect the shaping of the pieces.
With a long end of yarn and a darning needle, sew the sleeves into the armholes, spacing out the knitting for an even distribution of stitches along the sewing line.
Sew the underarm and side seams.
Fold the 5 stitch st.st edge of the neckline in half lengthwise (so it forms a little roll) and sew back onto itself.
Do the same with the 5 extra sts along the front edges, folding them over along the line of the 4th st.

hemlines

Fold up the hemline along the purl row, 6 rows from the bottom of the cardigan. Carefully stitch the cast-on edge to the row of purl sts that it naturally folds onto, ensuring your sewing stitches are not visible on the outside of the cardigan.
Repeat this process for the hemlines of the sleeves.

dyeing recipe

The yarn for the cardigan in the picture was immersion dyed (chapter 3) in one batch of 500 gr with Pale Pumpkin (yes, really!). After 10 minutes, a weak dye solution in Slate was poured on, with some light stirring after the first minute to ensure even distribution of the dye. There is still some colour variation in the yarn, which contributes to the stitch definition and gives a lovely depth to the colour. (see p. 25)

chunky socks

The starting point for these socks is 2 strands of regular sock yarn knitted together on thicker needles to create thicker, chunky socks to slob around in at home or keep feet toasty in walking boots or wellies.

Because the yarns used are proper sock yarns, they won't wear through at the heels or toes. You can substitute regular yarns, as long as you realise that the resulting socks are not suitable to be worn in shoes or boots.

The main body of the socks is knitted in a diamond and kite pattern that has a 12-stitch repeat. That works very well with these chunky socks but it can also be used with a single sock yarn knitted on 2.5 mm needles as you'll need 60 stitches, which is a multiple of 12.

about this pattern

difficulty

measurements
The number of stitches used is suitable to knit socks of sizes 3-4 and up

materials
150 - 200 grams of sock yarn depending on size

metreage needed
Approx. 600 – 800 metres (depending on size)

tension
20 sts and 27 rows measure 10 x 10 cm in stocking stitch

notions
One pair of 4 mm needles (if necessary, use bigger or smaller to achieve the right gauge).
Optional: 1 stitch holder and 2 stitch markers

stitches

diamond and kite: This is a combination of knit and purl stitches that is easy to knit and adds great texture to your socks. The pattern is a 24-round repeat, see below, rounds 1 – 24 under "leg".
stocking stitch: (st.st.) K on RS, P on WS
rib: K2, P2

cuff

Cast on 48 sts divided over 4 needles (12 sts per needle)
Rounds 1-16: Rib

leg

Rounds 1 & 2: *K6, P6, repeat from *
Rounds 3 & 4: *K5, P1, K1, P5, repeat from *
Rounds 5 & 6: *K4, [P1, K1] twice, P4, repeat from *
Rounds 7 & 8: *K3, [P1, K1] 3 times, P3, repeat from *
Rounds 9 & 10: *K2, [P1, K1] 4 times, P2, repeat from *
Rounds 11 & 12: *K1, P1, repeat from *
Rounds 13 & 14: *P1, K1, repeat from *
Rounds 15 & 16: *P2, [K1, P1] 4 times, K2, repeat from *
Rounds 17 & 18: *P3, [K1, P1] 3 times, K3, repeat from *
Rounds 19 & 20: *P4, [K1, P1] twice, K4, repeat from *
Rounds 21 & 22: *P5, K1, P1, K5, repeat from *
Rounds 23 & 24: *P6, K6, repeat from *

Repeat these 24 rounds to a total height of approx. 20 cm (8 in) or to your own preferred height – the point where you start the heel is just about where your ankle sticks out on the outside of your leg. Do make a note here which round of your 24-round repeat is the last row you've knitted as you will resume the pattern after knitting the heel.

heel

The heel is knitted with half of all sts (24), so only the sts on needles 1 and 2.
Leave the other sts on needles 3 and 4 OR transfer them to a stitch holder OR onto a spare piece of yarn in a contrasting colour

Row 1: S1, K29, turn
Row 2: S1, P29, turn
Continue in st.st on these 24 sts for 22 more rows
Row 25: S1, K13, SKPO, K1, turn
Row 26: S1, P5, P2tog, P1, turn
Row 27: S1, K to 1 st before the gap, SKPO, K1, turn
Row 28: S1, P to 1 st before the gap, P2tog, P1, turn
Repeat the last 2 rows until all the sts have been worked (14 sts)
Next row: K the 14 sts, then pick up and knit 10 sts from the heel flap, [place a stitch marker if you find it useful], knit the stitches on needles 3 and 4 in the diamond and kite pattern, picking up the pattern from the point where you interrupted it to knit the heel (transfer them onto the needles first if they've been on a stitch holder or a spare piece of yarn), [place another stitch marker], pick up and knit 10 sts up the other side of the heel flap, then knit 7 more sts (i.e. halfway through the 14 sts that form the bottom of the heel)
Note: needles 1 and 2 have 17 heel stitches each on them and needles 3 and 4 have 12 stitches each on them
Next round: K to 3 sts before the first stitch marker, K2tog, K1, K across needles 3 and 4 in the diamond and kite pattern (to the second stitch marker), K1, SKPO, K to end of round
Next round: K sts on needle 2, K diamond and kite on needles 3 and 4, K sts on needle 1
Repeat these last 2 rounds until you have 12 sts left on each needle (= 48 sts across all needles)

foot

Continue knitting round (needles 1 and 2 K, needles 3 and 4 diamond and kite) until you reach the desired length, which is the measurement of the foot from the heel to the tip of the big toe, minus 5 cm (2 in).
Now K 1 complete round in K sts only.

toe

Next round, starting at the beginning of needle 1: [K1, SKPO, K to 3 sts before the end of needle 2, K2tog, K1], repeat this across needles 3 and 4
Do check that you are decreasing your stitches in the correct places, i.e. to the sides of your toes, not on top and underneath!
Next round: K
Repeat these 2 rounds until you have 20 sts remaining (5 per needle)
Cast-off either using the kitchener stitch, or the 3-needle cast off method (see p. 94).

Weave in all loose ends or cast on the next sock first to avoid "second sock syndrome"!
(a familiar ailment amongst sock knitters, its most common symptom being a sudden and strong urge NOT to knit the second sock.)

dyeing recipe

Each hank was dyed in a dish (chapter 2) in the microwave with 2 different colours.
Hank 1: Plum and Pale Pumpkin
Hank 2: Slate and Stone
Note: Be careful not to squish the Pumpkin and Plum too much, as the Plum will completely dominate the Pumpkin if you mix them up a lot.

If you are looking for a real
challenge... turn the page

knitted clock face

A nice challenge for all you sock knitters. This project makes a fantastic present: very special, easy to personalise and (especially when given to a knitting-soulmate) about as impressive as you can make it.

I designed this cover to fit a simple Ikea clock called "Redo" but it can just as easily be used to cover a different clock. Redo is a metal clock with a slight dome shape to its face and the hands run with plenty of clearance from the face so you don't run the risk of getting them caught in the knitting.

The diameter of the clock is 28 cm (11 in) and it has one of these super-easy mechanisms that allow you to take off the hands simply by gently pulling them up and off the centre of the dial. So once you've knitted the cover, you simply remove the hands, slip the cover on and replace the hands. It really is as easy as that. If you're using a different clock from the Redo, the key things to look out for when assessing its suitability are the clearance of the hands from the clock face and whether the hands can be removed to slip the cover in position.

about this pattern

difficulty

measurements
The finished piece is a knitted circle with a diameter of 30 cm (12 in)

materials
Tall Yarns superwash 100% BFL (= Blue Faced Leicester, a breed of sheep) sock wool or a sock yarn of your choice

metreage needed
Approx. 240 m

tension
34 sts and 54 rows in st.st. measure 10 x 10 cm

notions
two sets of 2.0 mm double pointed needles (DPN's). (if necessary, use bigger / smaller to achieve gauge). It is easiest to work with 7 needles in total.

stitches

stocking stitch: As you're only knitting in the round, you only have to knit K stitches

thepattern

Cast on 6 sts , divide over 3 needles and join in the round.

Round 1: K
Round 2: [K1, M1] x 6 (12 sts)
Round 3: [K2, M1] x 6 (18 sts)
Round 4: [M1, K6] x 3 (21 sts)
Round 5: K
Round 6: K4, [M1, K7] x 2, M1, K3 (24 sts)

Now divide the sts over 6 needles (4 sts per needle)
Mark the start of a row either by placing a stitch marker or by pulling a small piece of scrap yarn (preferably in a contrasting colour) through the link between the last st on needle 6 and the first st on needle 1. This is an easier way of marking the start of a new row than placing a stitch marker while you're fiddling with a small number of sts on 6 needles.

Round 7: needles 1, 3, 5: M1, K4, M1 – needles 2, 4, 6: K (30 sts)
Round 8: needles 1, 3, 5: K – needles 2, 4, 6: M1, K4, M1 (36 sts)
Round 9: K
Round 10: [M1, K6] x 6 (42 sts)
Round 11: K
Round 12: needles 1, 3, 5: [M1, K7, M1] – needles 2, 4, 6: K (48 sts)
Round 13: needles 1, 3, 5: K – needles 2, 4, 6: [M1, K7, M1] (54 sts)
Round 14: [M1, K9] x 6 (60 sts)
Round 15: [M1, K10] x 6 (66 sts)
Round 16: K
Round 17: needles 1, 3, 5: [M1, K11, M1] – needles 2, 4, 6: K (72 sts)
Round 18: needles 1, 3, 5: K – needles 2,4,6: [M1, K11, M1] (78 sts)
Round 19: K
Round 20: [M1, K13] x 6 (84 sts)
Round 21: needles 1, 3, 5: [M1, K14, M1] – needles 2, 4, 6: K (90 sts)
Round 22: needles 1, 3, 5: K – needles 2, 4, 6: [M1, K14, M1] (96 sts)

You now have 16 sts on each needle.

Round 23: needles 1, 3, 5: [M1, K16, M1] – needles 2, 4, 6: K (102 sts)
Round 24: needles 1, 3, 5: K – needles 2, 4, 6: [M1, K16, M1] (108 sts)
Round 25: [M1, K18] x 6 (114 sts)
Round 26: K
Round 27: needles 1, 3, 5: [M1, K19, M1] – needles 2, 4, 6: K (120 sts)
Round 28: needles 1, 3, 5: K – needles 2, 4, 6: [M1, K19, M1] (126 sts)
Round 29: K
Round 30: [M1, K21] x 6 (132 sts)
Round 31: needles 11, 3, 5: [M1, K22, M1] – needles 2, 4, 6: K (138 sts)
Round 32: needles 1, 3, 5: K – needles 2, 4, 6: [M1, K22, M1] (144 sts)
Round 33: K
Round 34: [M1, K24] x 6 (150 sts)
Round 35: needles 1, 3, 5: [M1, K25, M1] – needles v: K (156 sts)
Round 36: needles 1, 3, 5: K – needles 2, 4, 6: [M1, K25, M1] (162 sts)
Round 37: K
Round 38: [M1, K27] x 6 (168 sts)

Round 39: K
Round 40: needles 1, 3, 5: [M1, K28, M1] – needles 2, 4, 6: K (174 sts)
Round 41: needles 1, 3, 5: K – needles 2, 4, 6: [M1, K28, M1] (180 sts)
Round 42: K
Round 43: needles 1, 3, 5: [M1, K30, M1] – needles 2, 4, 6: K (186 sts)
Round 44: needles 1, 3, 5: K – needles 2, 4, 6: [M1, K30, M1] (192 sts)
Round 45: K - you now have 32 sts on each needle
Round 46: needles 1, 3, 5: [M1, K32, M1] – needles 2, 4, 6: K (198 sts)
Round 47: needles 1, 3, 5: K – needles 2, 4, 6: [M1, K32, M1] (204 sts)
Round 48: needles 1, 3, 5: [M1, K34, M1] – needles 2, 4, 6: K (210 sts)
Round 49: needles 1, 3, 5: K – needles 2, 4, 6: [M1, K34, M1] (216 sts)
Round 50: K
Round 51: needles 1, 3, 5: [M1, K36, M1] – needles 2, 4, 6: K (222 sts)
Round 52: needles 1, 3, 5: K – needles 2, 4, 6: [M1, K36, M1] (228 sts)
Round 53: K
Round 54: [M1, K38] x 6 (234 sts)
Round 55: needles 1, 3, 5: [M1, K39, M1] – needles 2, 4, 6: K (240 sts)
Round 56: needles 1, 3, 5: K – needles 2, 4, 6: [M1, K39, M1] (246 sts)
Round 57: needles 1, 3, 5: [M1, K41, M1] – needles 2, 4, 6: K (252 sts)
Round 58: needles 1, 3, 5: K – needles 2, 4, 6: [M1, K41, M1] (258 sts)
Round 59: K
Round 60: needles 1, 3, 5: [M1, K43, M1] – needles 2, 4, 6: K (264 sts)
Round 61: needles 1, 3, 5: K – needles 2, 4, 6: [M1, K43, M1] (270 sts)
Round 62: needles 1, 3, 5: [M1, K45, M1] – needles 2, 4, 6: K (276 sts)
Round 63: needles 1, 3, 5: K – needles2, 4, 6: [M1, K45, M1] (282 sts)
Round 64: K - you now have 47 sts on each needle
Round 65: needles 1, 3, 5: [M1, K47, M1] – needles 2, 4, 6: K (288 sts)
Round 66: needles 1, 3, 5: K – needles 2, 4, 6: [M1, K47, M1] (294 sts)
Round 67: K
Round 68: [M1, K49] x 6 (300 sts)
Round 69: K
Round 70: needles 1, 3, 5: [M1, K50, M1] – needles 2, 4, 6: K (306 sts)
Round 71: needles 1, 3, 5: K – needles 2, 4, 6: [M1, K50, M1] (312 sts)
Round 72: needles 1, 3, 5: [M1, K52, M1] – needles 2, 4, 6: K (318 sts)
Round 73: needles 1, 3, 5: K – needles 2, 4, 6: [M1, K52, M1] (324 sts)
Round 74 - 79: K - you now have 54 sts on each needle
Round 80: K 3 sts together at the start of each needle (52 sts p. needle)
Round 81: as row 80 - you now have 50 sts on each needle
Round 82: [(K3tog, K10) x 3, K3tog, K9] x 6

Next round: cast-off all sts. Leave about 1 m (4 ft) of thread at the end. Weave this all round the cast-off edge, so the edge can be pulled tight once it is stretched over the clock face.

embroidering the numbers

On the clock in the picture the numbers are embroidered on with the darkest shade of yarn but can be done with any shade of your choice, as long as you ensure that there is enough contrast to make them easy to read. The embroidery technique used is called "Swiss darning". Instead of long stitches or cross stitches, you follow the little v-shapes of the knitting stitches. Swiss darning, when applied carefully, can easily be mistaken for Intarsia, as the embroidered stitches end up looking like knitting stitches in a different colour. Since the knitting stitches on the clock face run in different directions, the charts are different for every number. The numbers are all depicted holding the work in the position that it will be in once on the clock face. So there are "panel-seams" running through the numbers 12 and 6. These affect the angle of the stitches. To compensate for this angle, the charts show angled lines. Since the stitches are embroidered following the lines of the knitting stitches, it is recommended that you hold the work with the centre of the clock face towards you and the panel you are embroidering away from you. In other words: for each number, hold the area you are working on in the 12 o'clock position (this is why the number 6 chart is upside down and the 9 and 3 are both pictured sideways).
Note: *before you start the embroidery, do make sure that you are not working too close to the edge of your knitting, or else your numbers will disappear around the edge of the clock face.*

finishing

First ensure that you do not have any long, loose ends hanging from the back of your work. If you do weave in any ends, make sure that you cannot see any of it on the right side of your work. Also check that you do not have any loose or uneven stitches anywhere on your work, since this will stand out enormously once the clock is put together. Loose stitches are easily corrected by pulling any excess thread to the back of the work and, if necessary, securing it with a couple of small stitches.

Once you are happy with the finished piece, slip stitch a thread around the cast-off edge of your knitting (this can be the long end you left dangling after casting off). Now simply remove the hands from the clock (if you are using the Ikea Redo, you literally pull them off – gently of course), slip the cover over the centre of the dial and pull the edge of your knitting around the edge of the clock. Secure your knitting by pulling tight the thread that you have stitched around the edge of your work and secure it by tying it on to its starting point. Replace the hands (and in the case of the Redo, the little covering stud in the centre) and it's time to admire your work.

dyeing recipe

The yarn in the picture was dyed by mixing colours as described in chapter 4. I rewound the hank into little hanks by winding it around the thumb and elbow of one arm (using my other hand to do the winding). To monitor the amount of yarn in each little hank, I counted the number of loops I wound around my arm. The little hanks need to get progressively bigger, to accommodate the fact that you are knitting a circle that increases in diameter:
Hank 1: 10 loops. Hank 2: 15 loops. Hank 3: 22 loops. Hank 4: 32 loops. Hank 5: 45 loops. Hank 6: 60 loops. Hank 7: 60 loops.
Put each hank in a small plastic microwavable bag. Number the bags before you start to keep track of what goes where. Bag 1 is going to contain the smallest hank of yarn with the colour you want in the centre of your clock. Bag 7 contains the largest hank and, in this case, the darkest colour. Pour some water in each bag to soak the yarn. While the yarn is soaking, you can make up your dye solutions: one 10 grams pot each of Plum and Spring Yellow (each diluted in 150 ml of water). You use these 2 solutions to make up 7 little pots of mixed dyes (I used small glasses for this).

Distribute the dye in the small glasses, approximately as follows*:
Glass 1: 2 tsp yellow, 2 drops plum
Glass 2: 1 tbs yellow, 1/2 tsp plum
Glass 3: 1 tbs yellow, 1 tsp plum
Glass 4: 4 tsp yellow, 2 tsps plum
Glass 5: 2 tbs yellow, 2 tbs plum
Glass 6: 1 tbs yellow, 3 tbs plum
Glass 7: 4 tbs plum

*the quantities given are approximate – just have fun creating a range of your choice. When you've soaked the yarn for half an hour, tip out the excess water from every bag and tip each glass of dye mixture into its associated bag. Gently squeeze each bag to distribute the dye mixture. Stand the bags upright in a medium size microwavable tray. Prop them upright with some scrunched-up paper towel or use a smaller bowl if they threaten to fall over. Microwave everything together for 6 minutes. Leave to cool down completely.

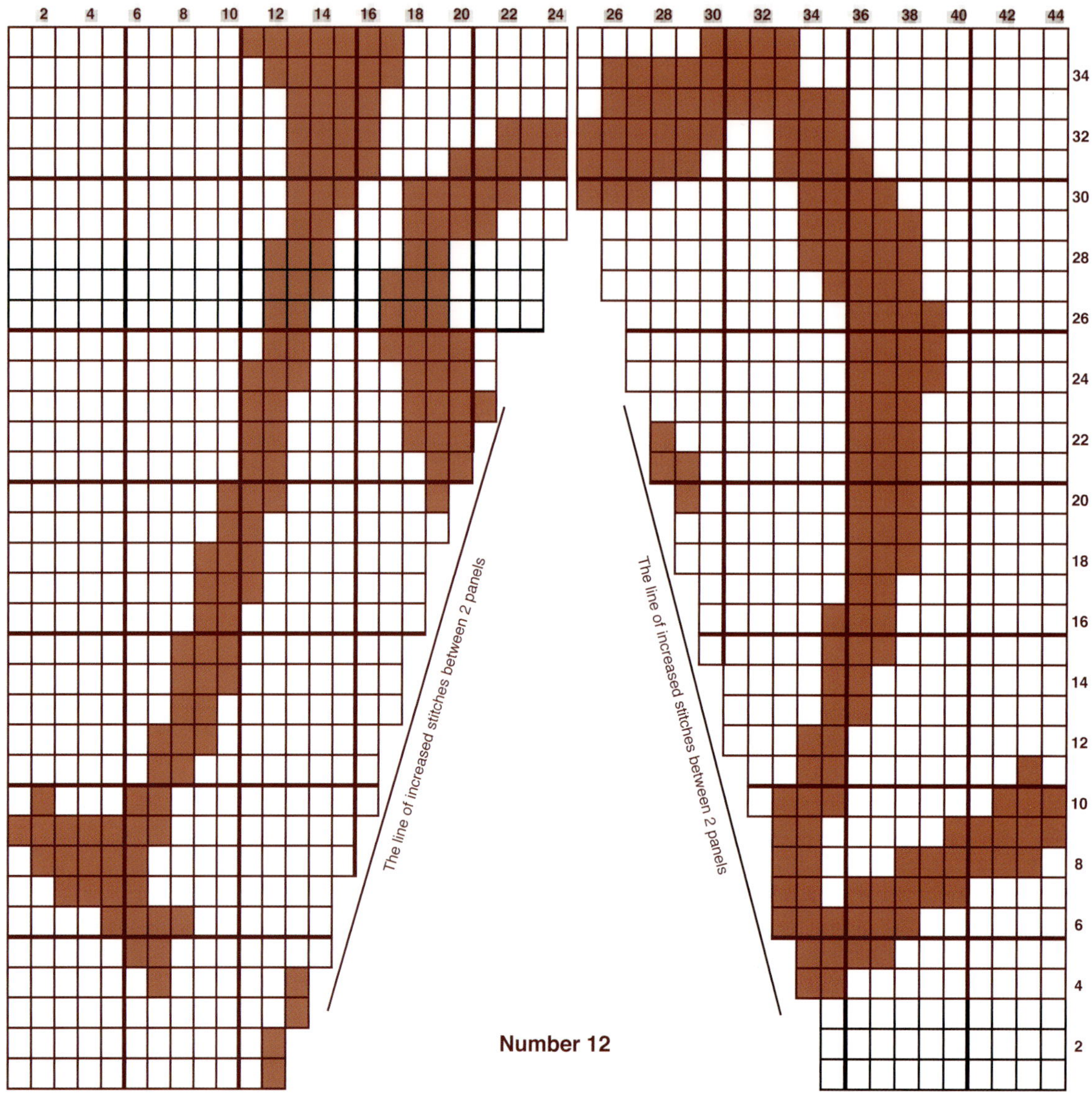

Number 12

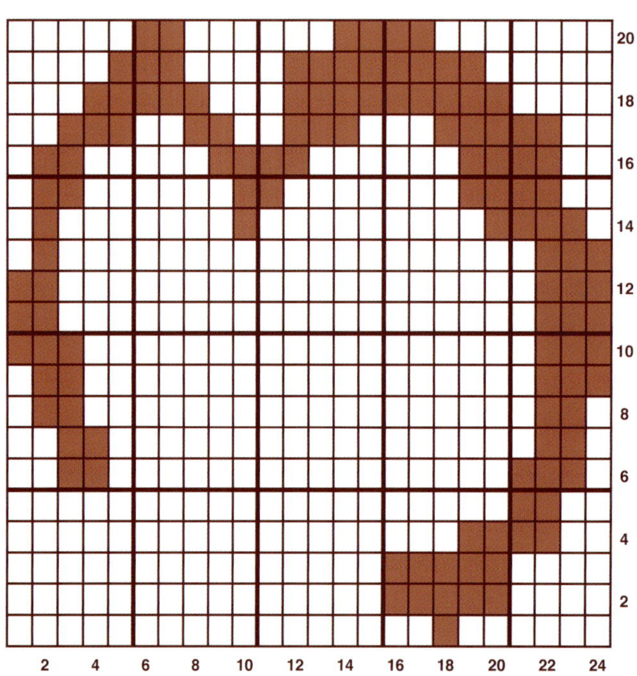

Number 3

Every square represents one knitting stitch (one little V-shape). Every coloured square is one knitting stitch covered with your chosen colour of embroidering thread.

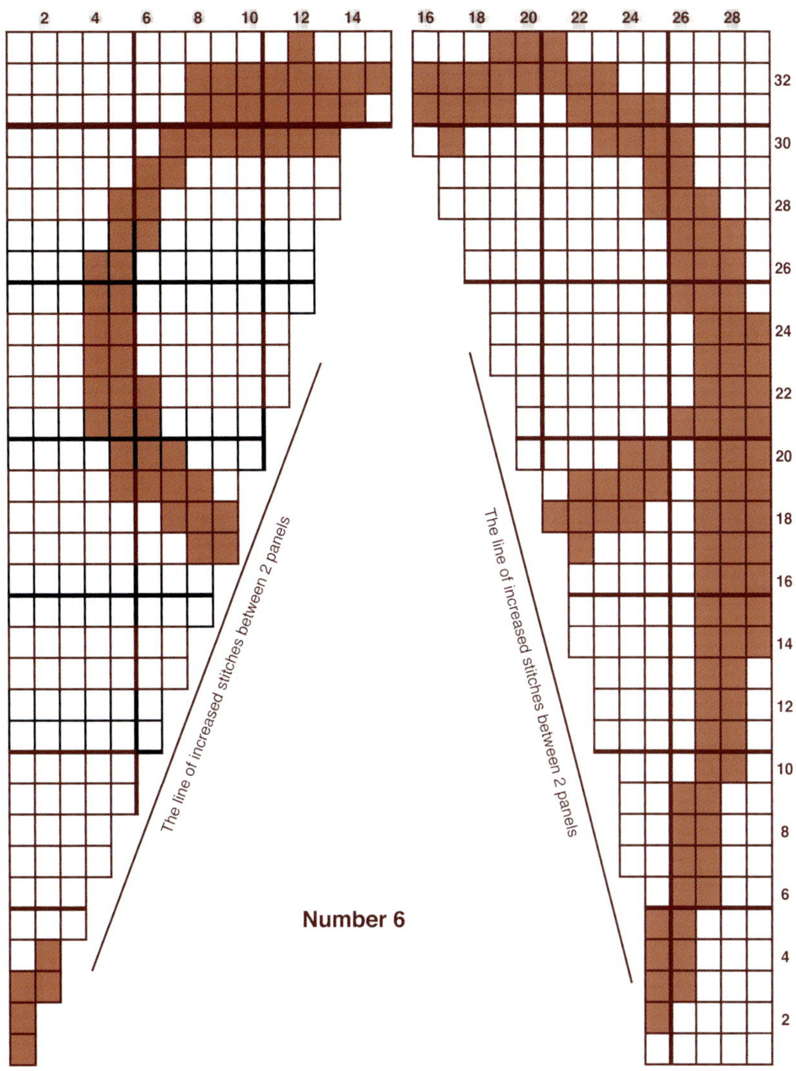

Number 6

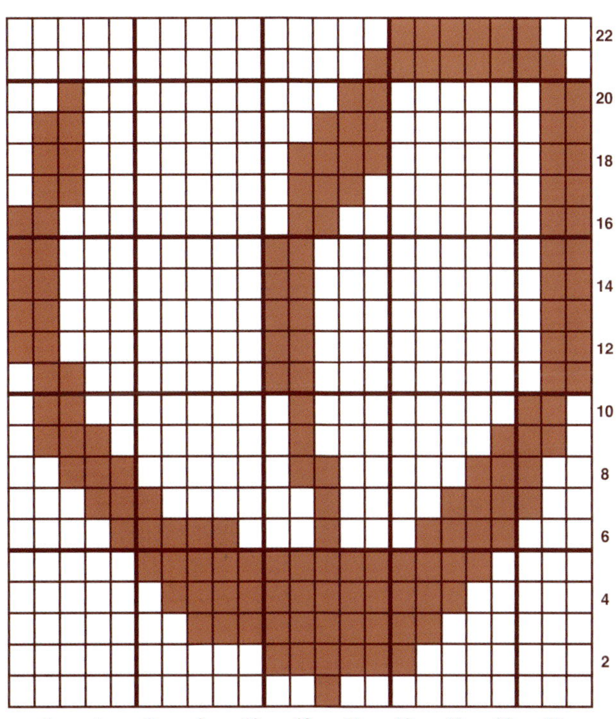

Number 9

useful stitches

Although this book teaches you to dye, not to knit, we have included a couple of stitches and techniques that you may find useful when working any of the patterns in the book. If you do come across a stitch or technique that we have not explained in detail, a quick search on the web will throw out a plethora of instructions, often with pictures or even video footage.

cable cast on

VERSION 1
Make a first st by making a slip knot on your left needle. Treat this as your first st. Insert the right needle into this st as if you are going to knit it, now knit it but do not drop it from the left needle. Instead, insert the left needle into the new st you have just created and slip it back off the right needle. You now have 2 sts on the left needle.
From this point, insert the right needle between the last 2 sts and repeat the above until you have the desired number of sts.

VERSION 2
As above, but from the point where you have 2 sts on the left needle, continue to insert the right needle into the last st (instead of in between the last 2 sts). This will result in a less robust but smoother cast-on edge.

three-needle cast off

This method is used to knit 2 pieces of knitting together, creating a seam between them. Please note that the resulting seam will not be flat but form a slight ridge, which makes it less suitable for the toe-seam on socks.

You start with 2 pieces of knitting, both still on the needles.
Hold the knitting with the right sides facing each other and the tips of the needles they are on facing in the same direction. Insert the tip of a third needle into the first stitch on the first needle, then into the first stitch on the second needle. Knit the two stitches together. Then again, *knit the first stitch from each needle together. Pass the previous stitch over this stitch as with a regular cast off. Repeat from *

kitchener stitch

This is often referred to as "real grafting" because, when done properly, your grafting yarn resembles a row of proper knitting stitches. And since you are sewing together 2 lines of stitches (not side by side but "head to head", as along a shoulder line or the toe of a sock), weaving the grafting yarn through them as if it were a line of knitting stitches ensures that the sewing line completely blends in.

Using the yarn that you have been knitting with, cut off a nice length (for a short graft of about 5 cm/2 in, a strand of 20 cm/8 in will do). Take a nice chunky darning needle and slide your end of yarn through it. Now follow the next steps:

ONE
(if your sts have not been cast off yet, e.g. in the case of a sock) Transfer your stitches onto 2 needles, one with the stitches that will sit on top of the foot, the other with the stitches from the sole. The needles will sit parallel, snugly side by side. Hold the needle that has the last stitch you knitted closest to you, as that will be the first needle you will work with.
(if your sts have been cast off, e.g. in the case of a shoulder line) Lay down the 2 pieces you are going to graft together flat and end to end, so the sts you are going to graft are facing each other.

TWO
Starting with the last stitch you knitted (or: at one end of your shoulder), slide the darning needle into the last stitch as if you were going to knit it, but instead, push the needle all the way through and drop the knitting stitch from the needle.

THREE
Now pass the darning needle through the next stitch on the same knitting needle (or same shoulder panel) but coming through from behind, i.e. as if you were to purl that stitch. Keep the stitch on the needle.

FOUR
Pass the darning needle through the first stitch on the back needle (or other shoulder panel) as if you were to purl that stitch. Drop the stitch off the needle. As you are working, don't pull the working thread too tight.

FIVE
Pass the darning needle through the second stitch on the back needle (or same shoulder panel) as if you were to knit that stitch. Keep the stitch on the needle.

SIX
Repeat steps 2 - 5 until all the stitches have been grafted together. If the yarn you've woven through is too loose and it looks like big knitting stitches, carefully pull it a bit tighter by working the yarn through the loops of your grafted stitches, one at a time. Weave in the end of your yarn and cut off any excess.

mattress stitch

Mattress stitch is ideal for neat side and sleeve seams. It is always done with the right side of the knitting facing you. Lay the pieces to be joined side by side. Start the seam at the bottom edge. First join the cast-on rows, inserting the needle between the first and second stitch in from the edge, underneath one of the "bars" of yarn that run between the stitches. Pick up one bar on the left piece of knitting, one on the right, etc., leaving the thread you are working with quite loose so you can easily see where you are. Keep going, one bar on the left, one on the right. If you are joining very fine knitting, you can consider picking up 2 bars at a time on each side but be careful not to work in big steps or your resulting seam will look messy. After 2 - 3 cm / 1 in of seam, pull the thread fast. You'll notice the sts from both pieces of knitting aligning very neatly. Your seam is virtually impossible to see on the outside. On the inside of your work, you will see the edge sts of both pieces running alongside each other like a neat ridge. With this method all patterns can be perfectly joined. In the seam the corresponding rows of the two pieces always come together. When combining stripes, intarsia, rib or lace, do take extra care to pick up the correct bars so the pattern/colour/motif continues from one panel onto the other.

i-cord

Cast on 3, 4, 5 or 6 sts, using double pointed needles. For the Fair Isle Bag pattern, cast on 4 sts. K one row, do not turn. Instead, *slip the sts back to the other side of the needle you've just knitted them onto. Knit them again. Repeat from * until you have a cord that is long enough. The first couple of rows feel awkward, as you keep pulling the yarn along the back of the work every time you start a new row. After a short length of knitting, pull down on the cord. This will help close the connection between the sts in the back, i.e. where you pull the yarn across when starting a new row. Once the cord is long enough, break off the yarn, leaving a 10 cm/4 in end. Thread the yarn through all sts. Pull tight.

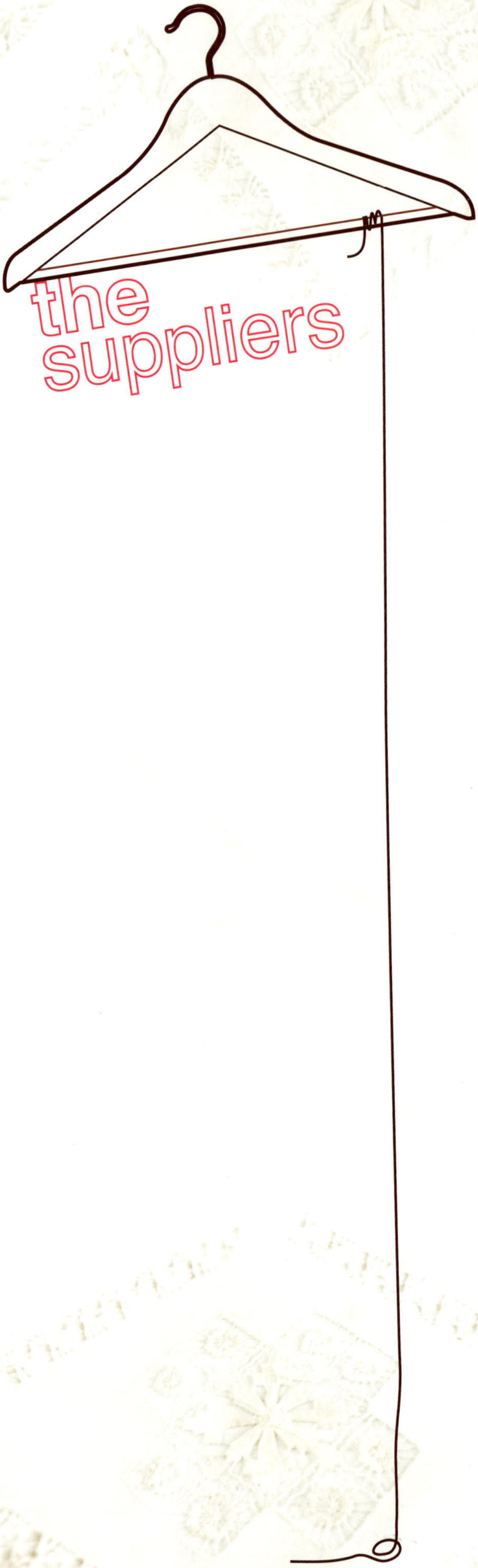

the suppliers

Most items used in the book can be bought online.

All-in-one Acid Dyes
4 primary colours
www.crosswayspatch.co.uk
12 colour collection
www.tallyarns.co.uk

All un-dyed yarns used in the book
www.tallyarns.co.uk

Bamboo and Knit-pro Symfonie knitting needles
www.tallyarns.co.uk

Buttons
www.injabulo.co.uk

Citric acid
www.brew-it-yourself.co.uk *or a pharmacy*

Darning needles
www.tallyarns.co.uk

Manutex
Kemtex Educational Supplies Ltd
www.kemtex .co.uk

Microwavable dishes
Kitchenware shops, or use any empty food-container (ice-cream tubs are great) as long as the plastic has a number 5 code on it)

Vintage knitting needles
Try your local charity shop

On our sites you can also find details of workshops, talks and our local knitting groups.
We can arrange classes, workshops, demonstrations and lectures at Helen's purpose-built workshop and studio.

Rose Glen
Crossways Road
Grayshott
Hindhead
Surrey GU26 6HG
e-mail: helen@crosswayspatch.co.uk
or linda@tallyarns.co.uk

Helen has published the following books to date:
Dyeing in plastic bags © 2001,
ISBN 978-0-9540333-1-6
Magic dyeing made easy © 2003,
ISBN 978-0-9540333-2-3
Textile coil pots © 2004,
ISBN 978-0-9540333-4-7
Beautiful braiding made easy © 2006,
ISBN 978-0-9540333-5-4

For more information, visit
www.crosswayspatch.co.uk